Fort Erie Ontario in Colour Photos, Saving Our History One Photo at a Time

Photography by Barbara Raué
©2018

Series Name: Cruising Ontario

Book 211: Fort Erie, Ridgeway, Stevensville

Cover photo: 202 Dufferin Street, Fort Erie, Page 11

©All the photos in this book have been taken with my cameras. I own the rights to them.

Series Name: Cruising Ontario
Saving Our History One Photo at a Time
in colour photos

Books Available in Alphabetical Order:
Aberfoyle, Acton, Ajax, Alton, Amherstburg, Ancaster, Arthur, Auburn, Aylmer, Ayr, Beaver Valley, Belgrave, Belleville, Bloomingdale, Blyth, Brantford, Brockville, Burford, Burlington, Caledon, Caledonia, Cambridge, Carlow, Chatsworth, Clifford, Collingwood, Conestogo, Delhi, Dorchester to Aylmer, Drayton, Drumbo, Dundas, Dunlop, Eden Mills, Elmira, Elora, Erin, Essex, Fergus, Goderich, Grimsby, Guelph, Hagersville, Hamilton, Hanover, Harriston, Hespeler, Jarvis, Kingston, Kingsville, Kitchener, Lake Superior, Lincoln, Linwood, Listowel, London, Lucknow, Merrickville, Mono, Mount Forest, Mount Pleasant, Neustadt, New Hamburg, Newboro, Newport, Niagara-on-the-Lake, Niagara Falls, North Bay, Oakville, Onondaga, Orangeville, Orillia, Oshawa, Owen Sound, Palmerston, Paris, Pelham, Perth, Peterborough, Petrolia, Pickering, Port Colborne, Port Elgin, Portland, Preston, Rockwood, Sarnia, Sault Ste. Marie, Seaforth, Sheffield, Shelburne, Simcoe, Smiths Falls, Smithville, Southampton, St. Catharines, St. George, St. Jacobs, St. Marys, St. Thomas, Stoney Creek, Stratford, Thamesford, Thunder Bay, Tillsonburg, Toronto, Waterdown, Waterford, Waterloo, Welland, Wellesley, West Flamborough, Westport, Whitby, Windsor, Wingham, Woodstock

Book 203: Ajax, Pickering
Book 204-206: Oshawa
Book 207-209: Niagara Falls
Book 210: North Bay
Book 211: Fort Erie

Table of Contents

Fort Erie   Page 7

    Jarvis Street

    Niagara Boulevard

    Dufferin Street

    Central Avenue

    350 Lakeshore Road

Ridgeway   Page 23

Stevensville   Page 39

Fort Erie is a town on the Niagara River in the Niagara Region of Ontario. It is across the river from Buffalo, New York and is the site of Old Fort Erie which played a prominent role in the War of 1812.

Fort Erie is also home to other commercial core areas of Bridgeburg, Ridgeway, Stevensville and Crystal Beach as a result of the 1970 amalgamation of Bertie Township and the village of Crystal Beach with Fort Erie.

The Fort Erie area contains deposits of flint, and became important in the production of spearheads, arrowheads, and other tools.

After the Treaty of Paris, which ended the French and Indian War and transferred Canada from France to Britain, King George III issued the Royal Proclamation of 1763 establishing the territory beyond which (including what is now Southern Ontario) would be an Indian Reserve. This was an attempt to avoid further conflict with the Indians, although it did not forestall Pontiac's War the following year. The British also built a string of military forts to defend their new territory, including Fort Erie, the first version of which was established in 1764.

During the American Revolution Fort Erie was used as a supply depot for British troops. After the war the territory of what is now the Town of Fort Erie was settled by soldiers demobilised from Butler's Rangers, and the area was named Bertie Township in 1784.

The original fort was located on the Niagara River's edge below the present fort. It served as a supply depot and a port for ships transporting merchandise, troops and passengers via Lake Erie to the Upper Great Lakes. The fort was damaged by winter storms and in 1803 plans were made for a new fort on the higher ground behind the original. It was larger and made of flint stone but was not quite finished at the start of the War of 1812.

During the war, the Americans attacked Fort Erie twice in 1812, captured and abandoned it in 1813, and then recaptured it in 1814. The Americans held it for a time, breaking a prolonged British siege. Later they destroyed Fort Erie and returned to Buffalo in the winter of 1814.

The Fort Erie area became a major terminus for slaves using the Underground Railroad between 1840 and 1860; many had crossed into Canada from Buffalo, New York.

In 1866, during the Irish-American Fenian raids, between 1,000 and 1,500 Fenians crossed the Niagara River, invading Canada as part of an attempt to oust the British and create an independent Irish republic; they occupied the town and demanded food and horses. The only payment they were able to offer was Fenian bonds which were not acceptable to the citizens. The Fenians then cut the telegraph wires and tore up some railway tracks. Afterwards, they marched to Chippewa and the next day to Ridgeway where they fought the Battle of Ridgeway, a series of skirmishes with the Canadian militia. The Fenians then returned to Fort Erie and fought the Battle of Fort Erie in 1866, defeating the Canadian militia. Fearing British reinforcements, they then decided to retreat to the U.S.

The Battle of Ridgeway shocked the country, spurring improvements to Canada's defences, and helping to bolster the movement for confederation, which took place the next year.

Ridgeway takes its name from the limestone ridge which runs through it from north to south. The main street of town aptly named Ridge Road, follows this ridge, and was part of one of the first two wagon trails in Bertie Township, connecting Point Abino on Lake Erie to Miller's Creek on the Niagara River.

Ridgeway was settled by the United Empire loyalists in the late 18th-century, and was originally a farming community. In the 1850s the Buffalo, Brantford and Goderich Railway line was put through, and service industries began to develop around the train stop on Ridge Road. The business district spread north from there towards Dominion Road. In 1873 the post office was opened, having been moved from Point Abino.

In 1869 Fort Erie was served by the Grand Trunk and the Erie & Niagara railways. The Grand Trunk Railway built the International Railway Bridge in 1873, bringing about a new town, originally named Victoria and subsequently renamed to Bridgeburg, north of the original settlement of Fort Erie. By 1876, Ridgeway had a population of about 800, the village of Fort Erie had about 1,200, and Victoria had three railway stations. By 1887, Stevensville had a population of about 600, Victoria of about 700, Ridgeway of about 600, and Fort Erie of about 4,000.

Situated a few kilometres north of Lake Erie, and a short drive from Niagara Falls, Stevensville is surrounded primarily by agricultural land. The centre of the community is the intersection of Stevensville Road and Main Street. Black Creek runs through the area which is often used for kayaking and canoeing, with a boat launch at the end of Main Street.

In 1888, the amusement park at Crystal Beach opened. The park continued to operate until it closed in 1989.

On August 7, 1927 the Peace Bridge was opened between Fort Erie and Buffalo.

Fort Erie

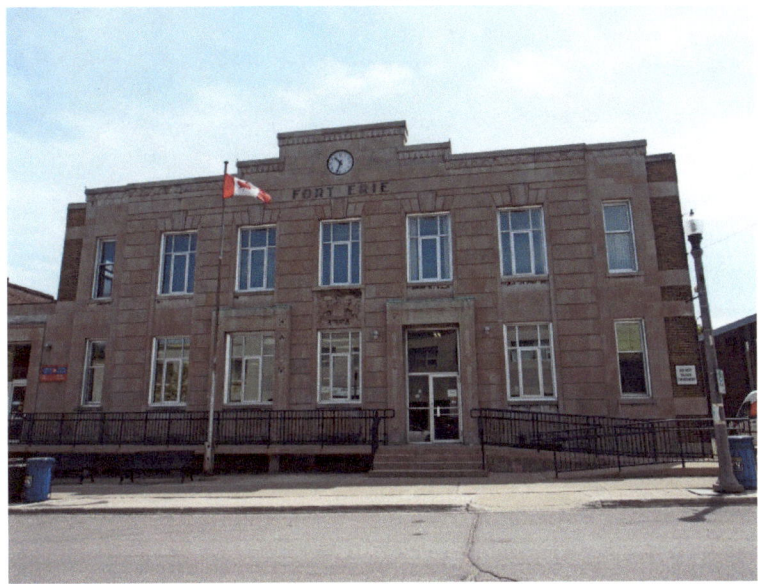

55 Jarvis Street – Fort Erie Post Office

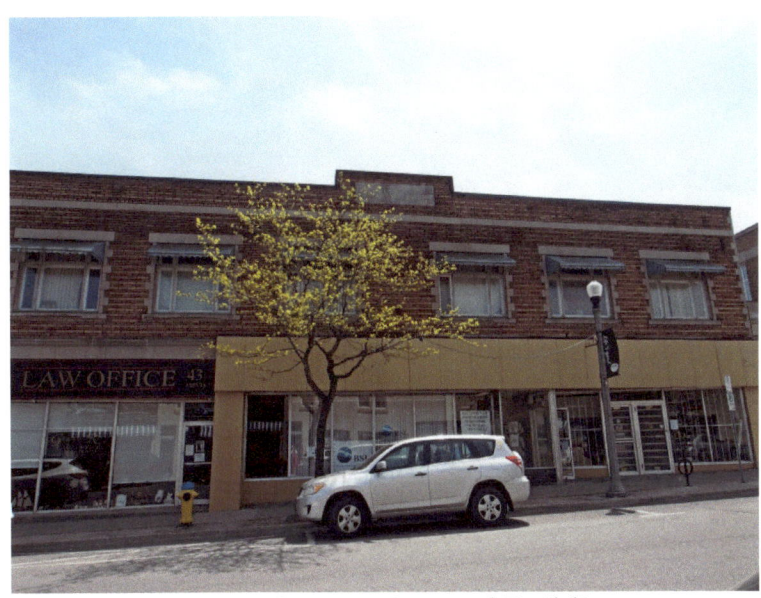

43 Jarvis Street – Atwood Building

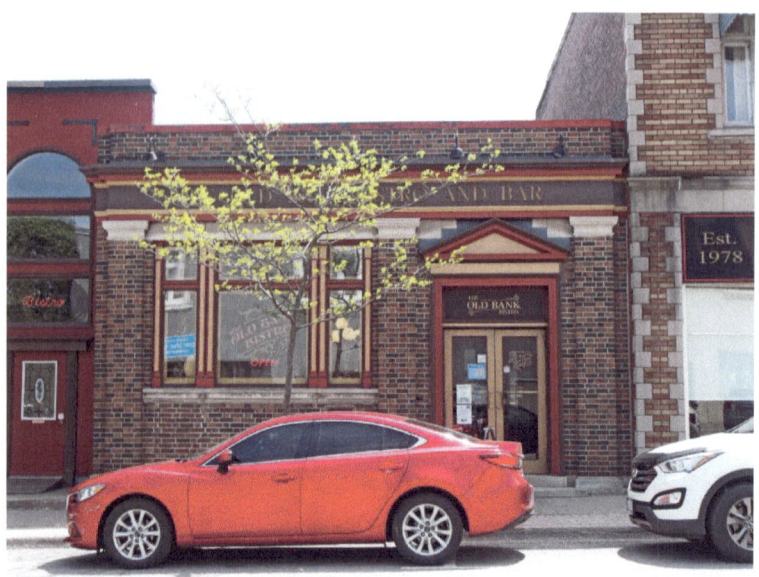

41 Jarvis Street – Built in 1924, the original Bank of Montreal serviced the town of Bridgeburg (as it was known then) until a new larger facility was built in 1967. The Old Bank Bistro Restaurant opened in 2005.

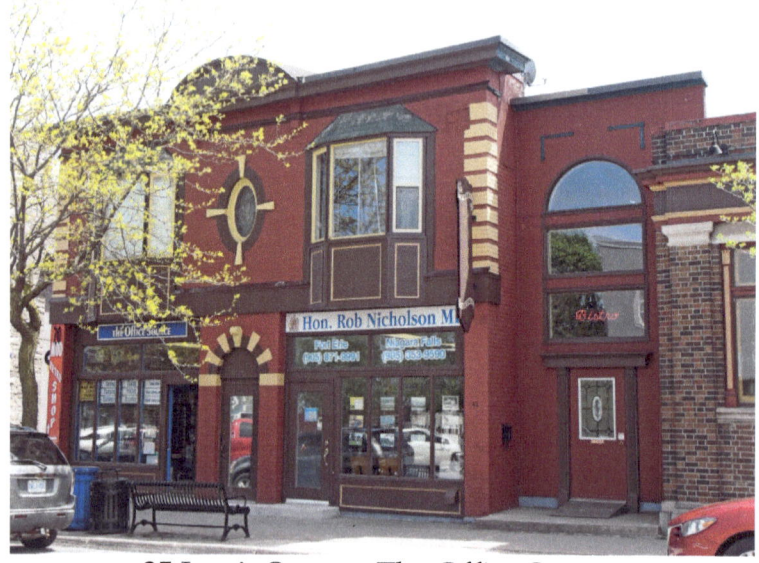

35 Jarvis Street – The Office Source

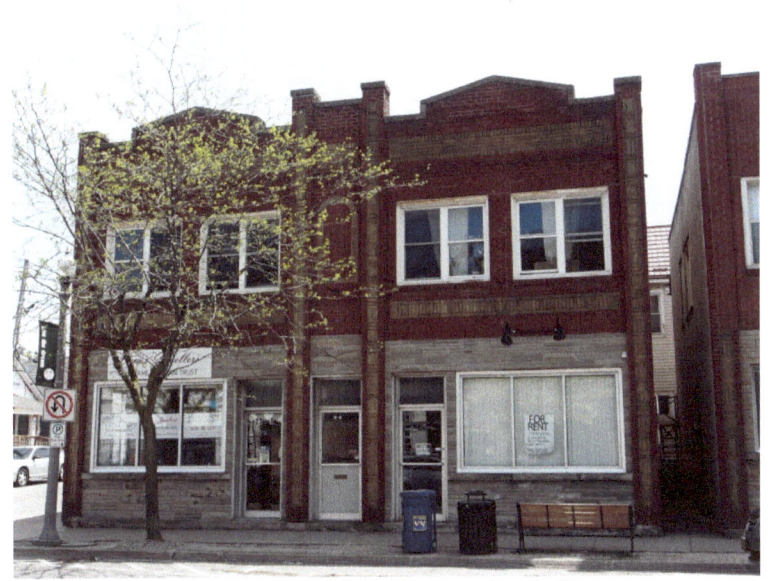

23 Jarvis Street – Venus Jewellers

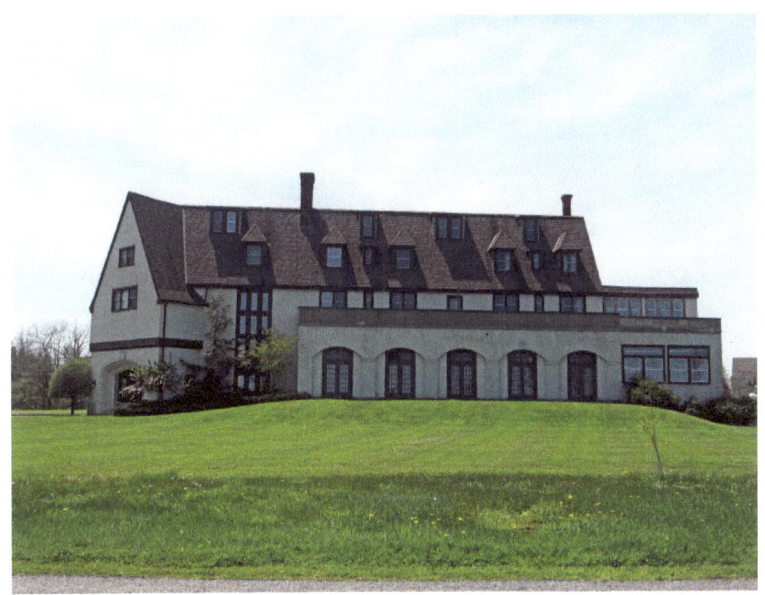

Niagara Boulevard – Niagara Christian Collegiate

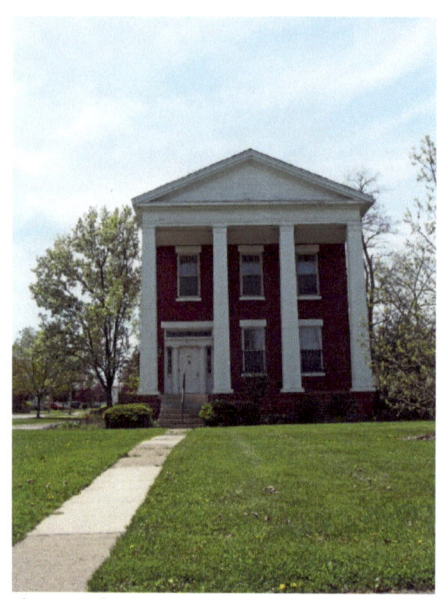

657 Niagara Boulevard – Forsyth-Pattison-Kilbridge (Bertie Hall) – built in 1832 – was part of the Underground Railroad known for helping slaves to their freedom in Canada.

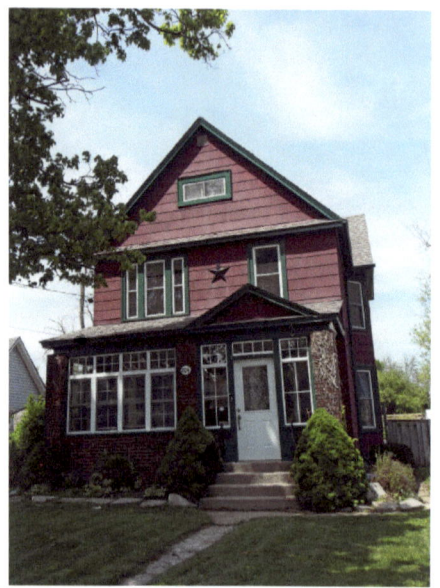

204 Dufferin Street

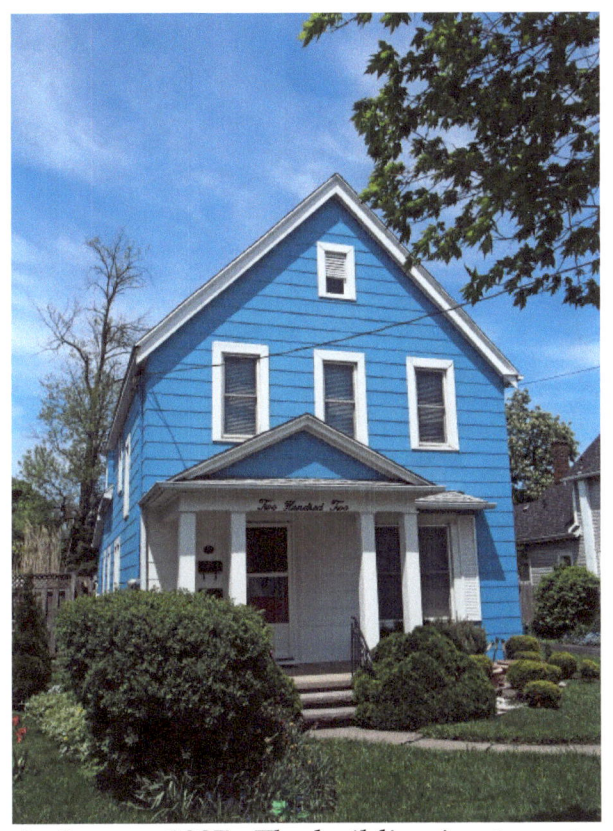

202 Dufferin Street – 1897 - The building is a two-story, single detached home featuring a front gable design with a steep pitched roof in Gothic style. The main entry has a pedimented portico supported by two paired pilasters. The wooden clapboard exterior is painted Henley Blue and the six inch wide window trim, which surrounds the single pane double hung windows, stands in marked contrast.

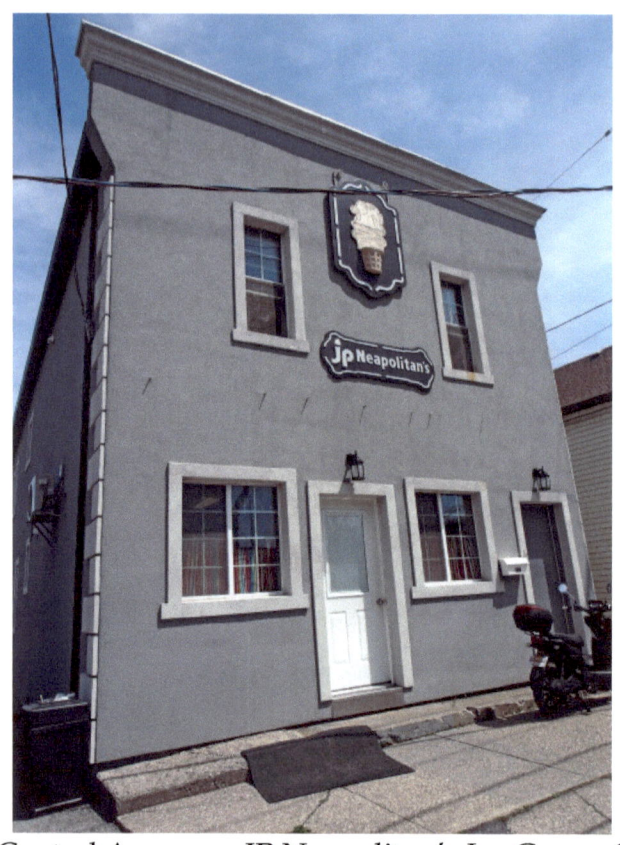

566 Central Avenue – JP Neapolitan's Ice Cream Shop

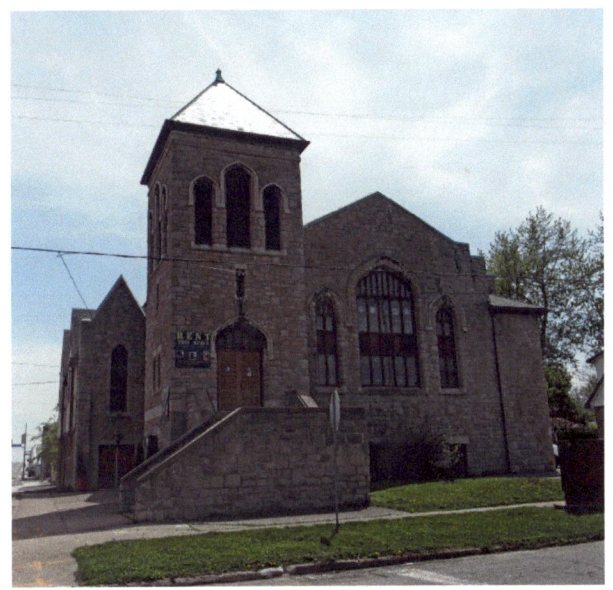

575 Central Avenue - This former church, now called The Bell Tower has been repurposed to provide a place for meetings. In the Main Event Room is the venue for comedy shows, live bands and Karaoke for kids and adults.

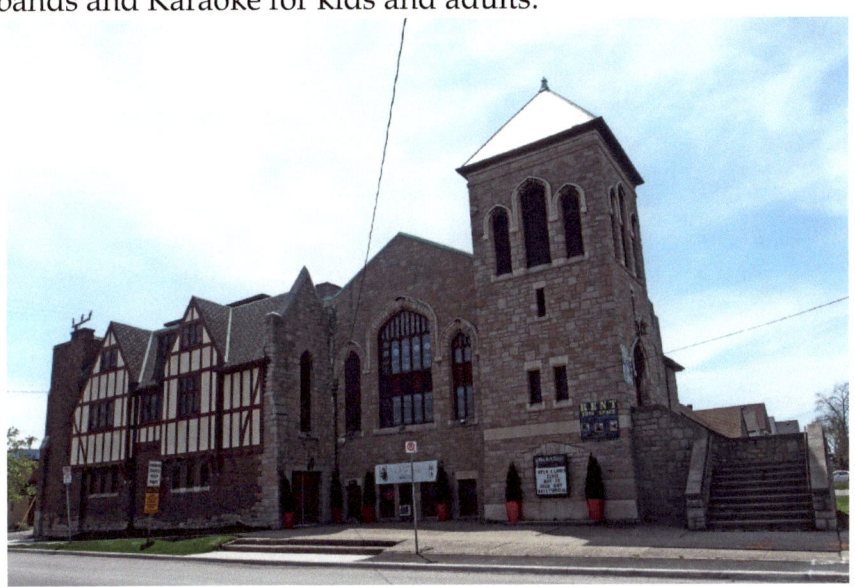

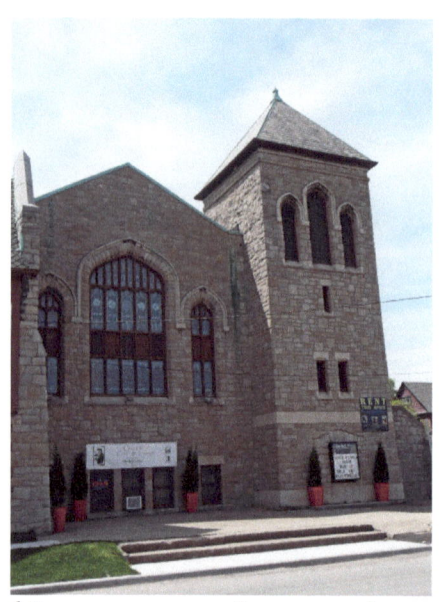

Quasi's Café and Lounge serves homemade meals and fresh-baked bread for lunch and dinner. The Gallery houses the art of various local artists. It has been used for weddings, celebrations of life, small corporate meetings, poetry nights and jazz ensembles.

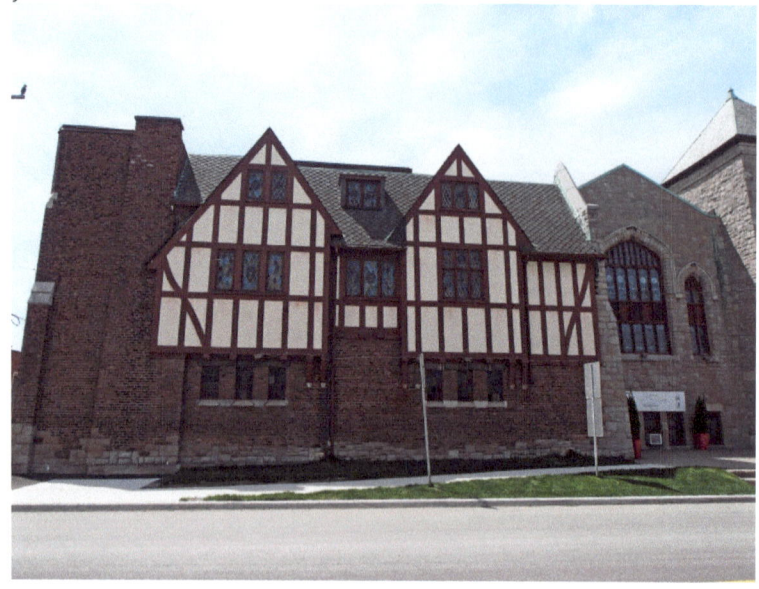

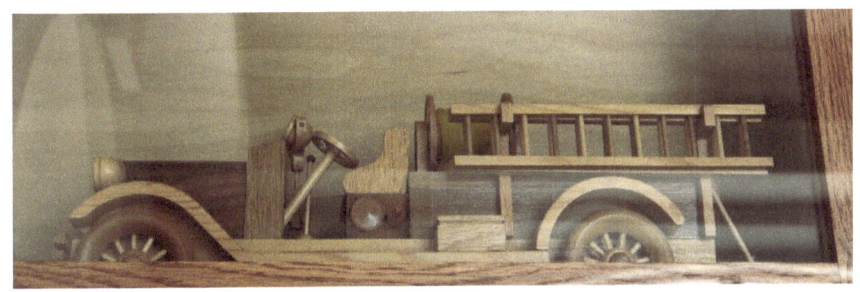

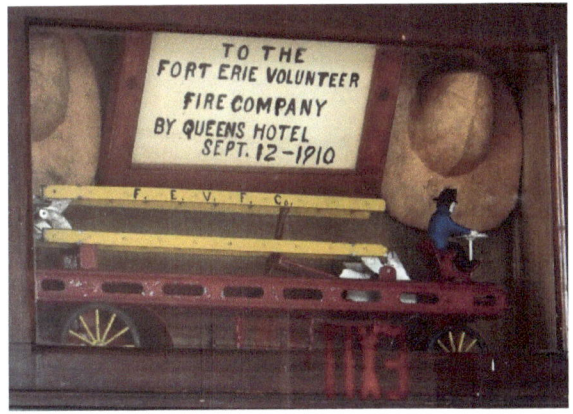

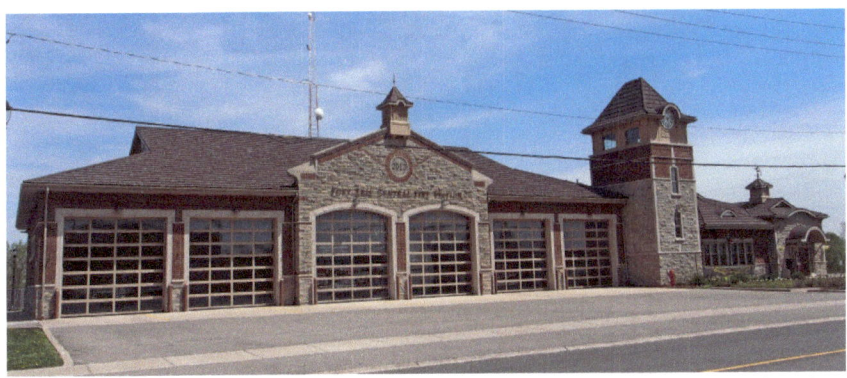

444 Central Avenue – Fort Erie Central Fire Station - 2013

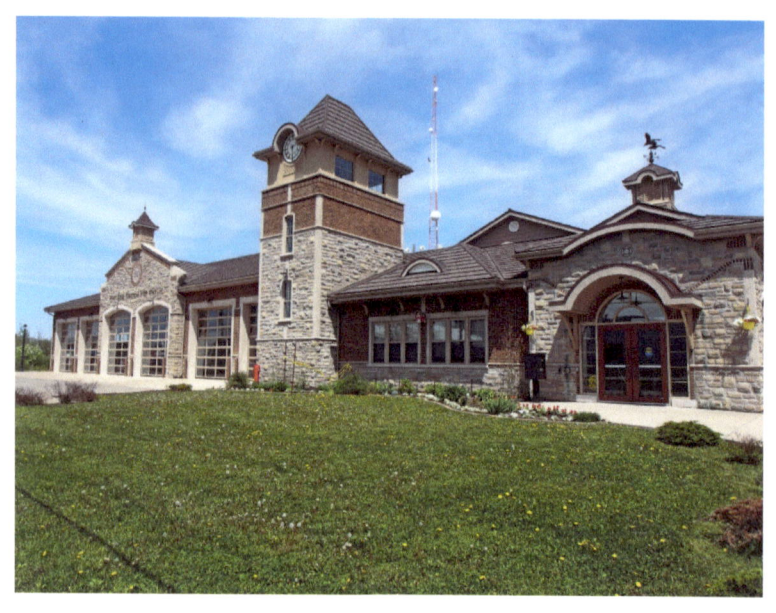

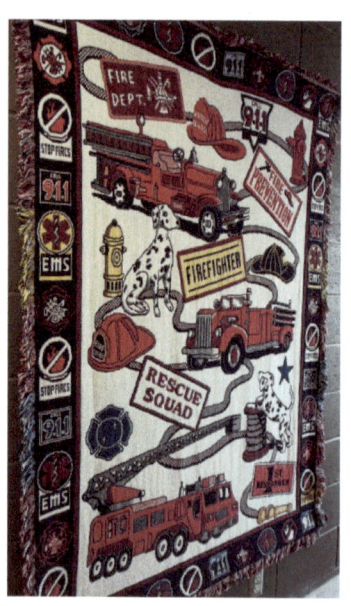

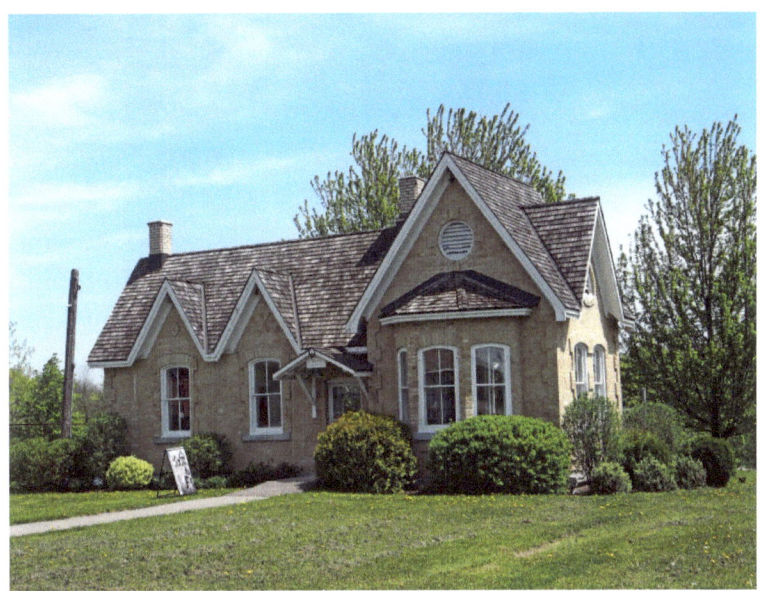

The B-1 Grand Trunk Station was built in 1873 by the Grand Trunk Railway to coincide with the construction of the International Railway Bridge. The B-1's companion station, the B-2 was located in Black Rock, New York on the American side of the bridge.

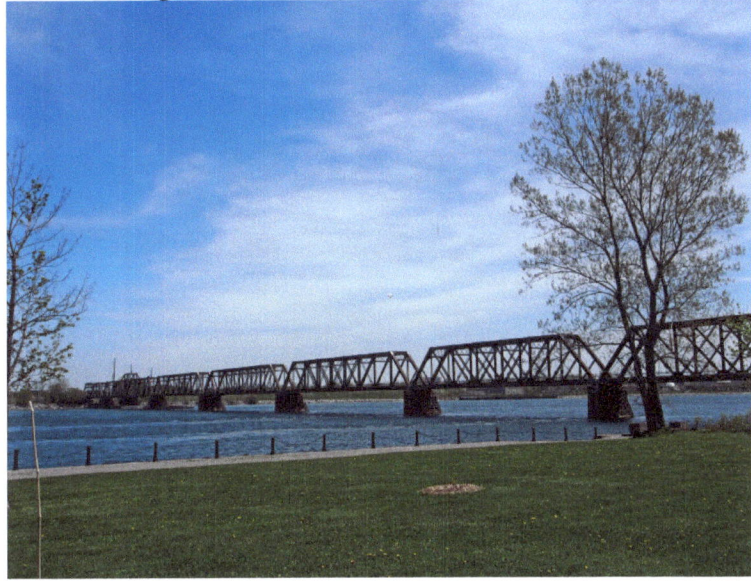

The International Railway Bridge spans the Niagara River to accommodate rail traffic. The engineers had to deal with treacherous currents, fluctuating water levels, and ice floes. Station operators at the B-1 station kept records of rail traffic and maintenance work, water depth at each pier, weather, and boats passing under the bridge.

The International Railway Bridge played a significant role in the history of Fort Erie and was one of the main entry points across the country of rail freight from the United States. The bridge is still in use today without the use of the stations.

The B-1 station fell into disuse; it was restored and opened in 1984 as the Fort Erie Railroad Museum at 400 Central Avenue.

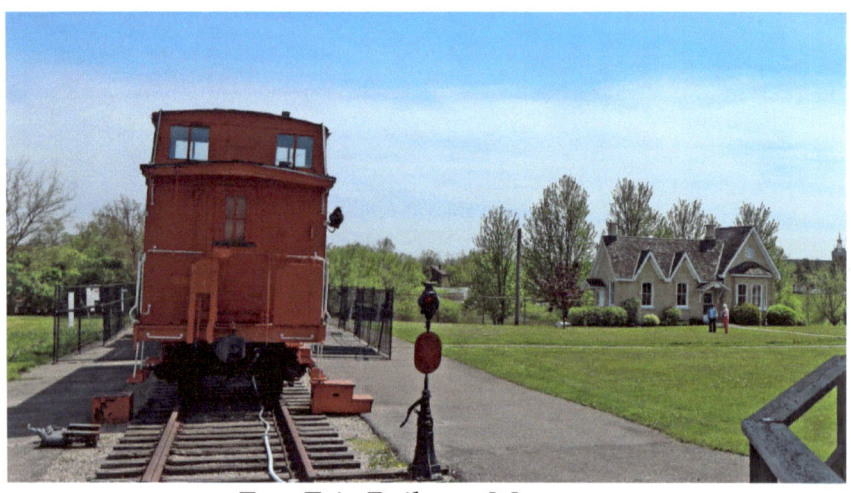

Fort Erie Railway Museum

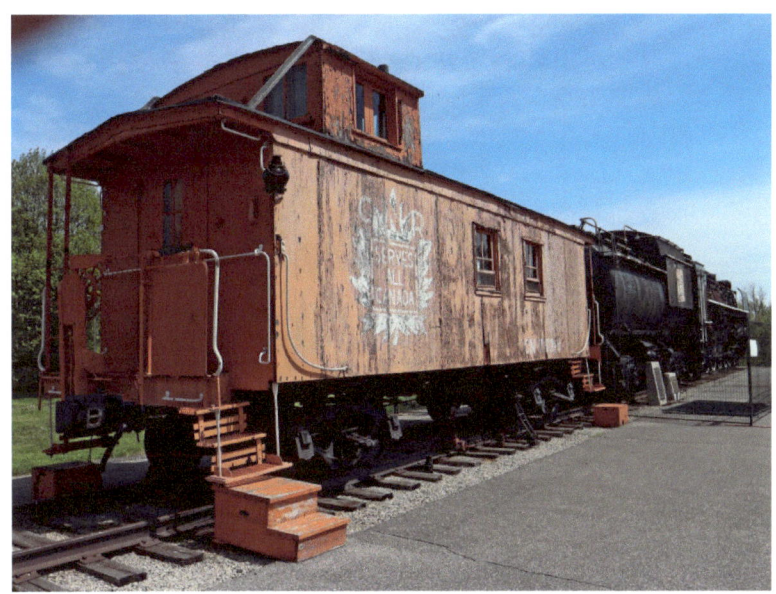

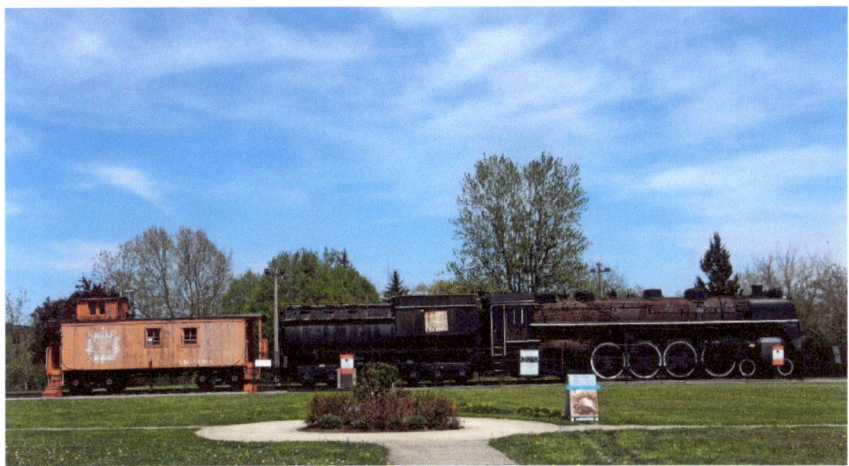

CN 6218 Steam Engine - Built in 1948, the 4-8-4 wheel configuration Northern type served well into the 1960s. In its retirement it serves as a reminder of days past when Fort Erie boasted the third-largest rail yard in Canada.

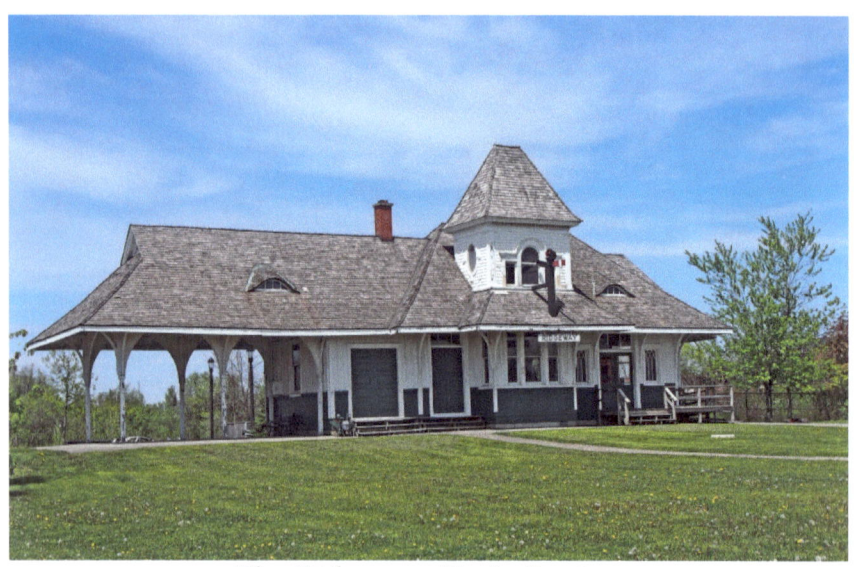
The Ridgeway Train Station

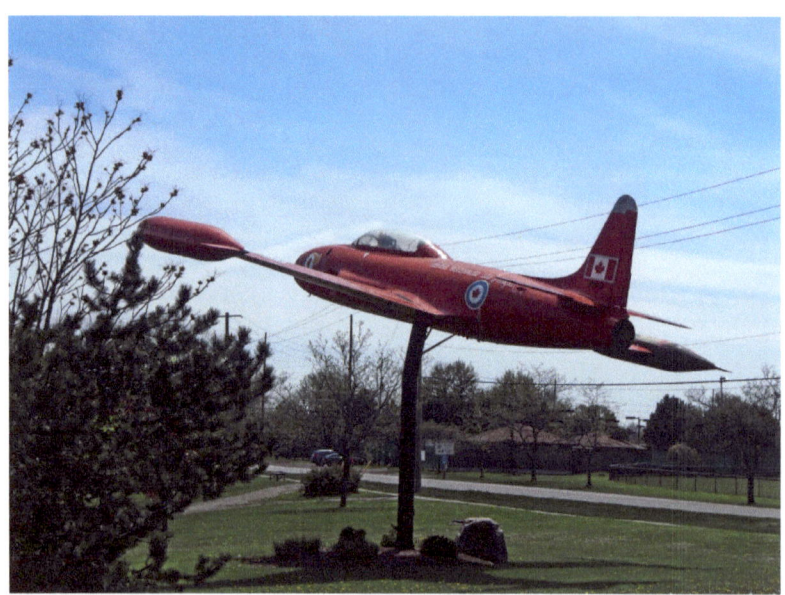
R.C.A.F. "Red Knight" T33 Jet Aircraft was built by Canadair in 1954

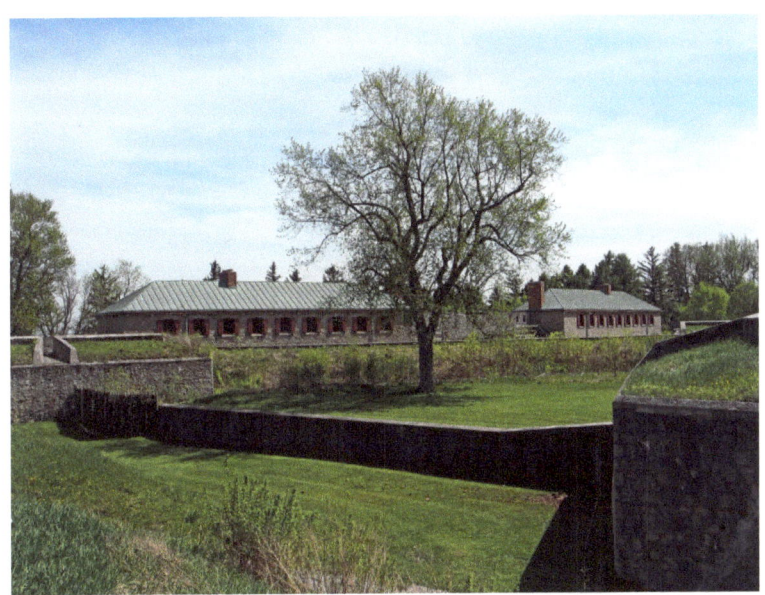

350 Lakeshore Road - Fort Erie was the first British fort to be constructed as part of a network developed after the Seven Years' War was concluded by the Treaty of Paris at which time all of New France was ceded to Great Britain. 3 foot thick fieldstone curtain walls and foundations of the fort surviving from the 1812-1814 period form part of the current exterior walls.

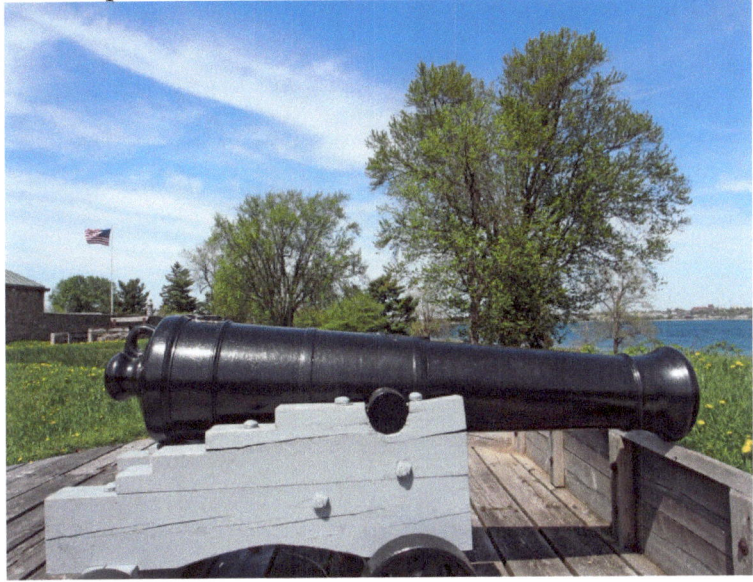

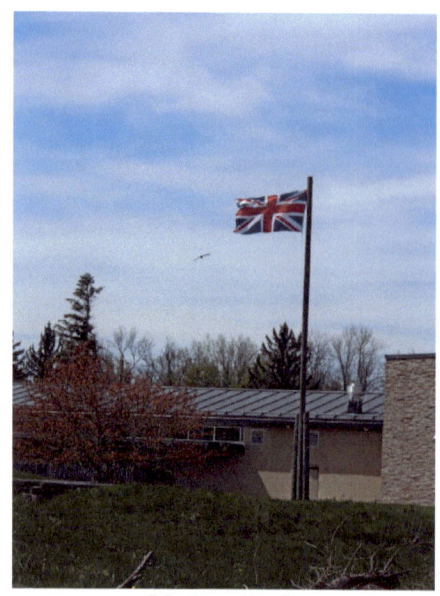
Union Jack

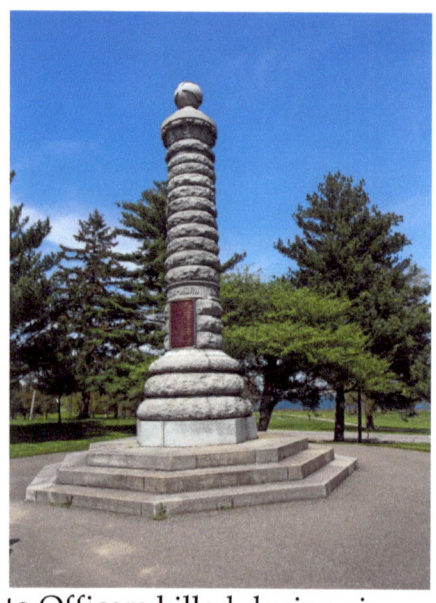
Memorial to Officers killed during siege of Fort Erie

Ridgeway

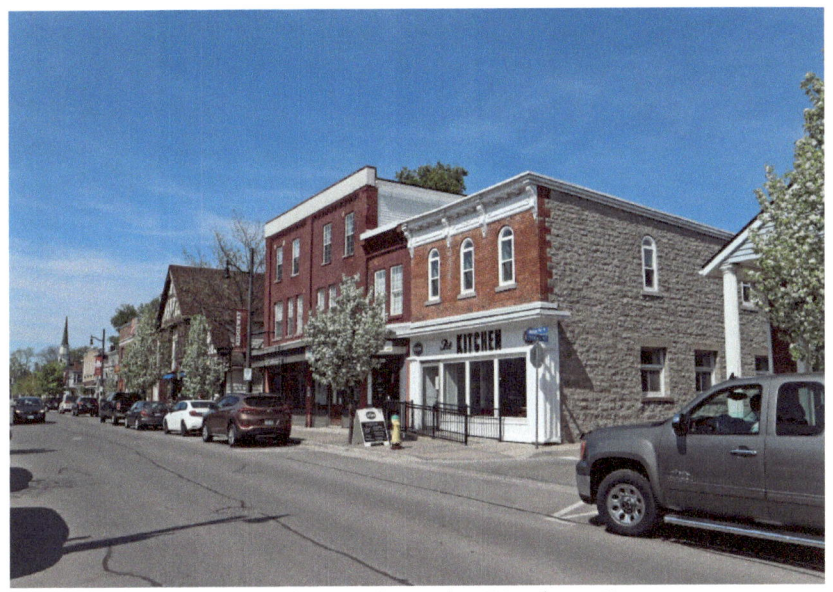

294 Ridge Road North – The Kitchen Restaurant

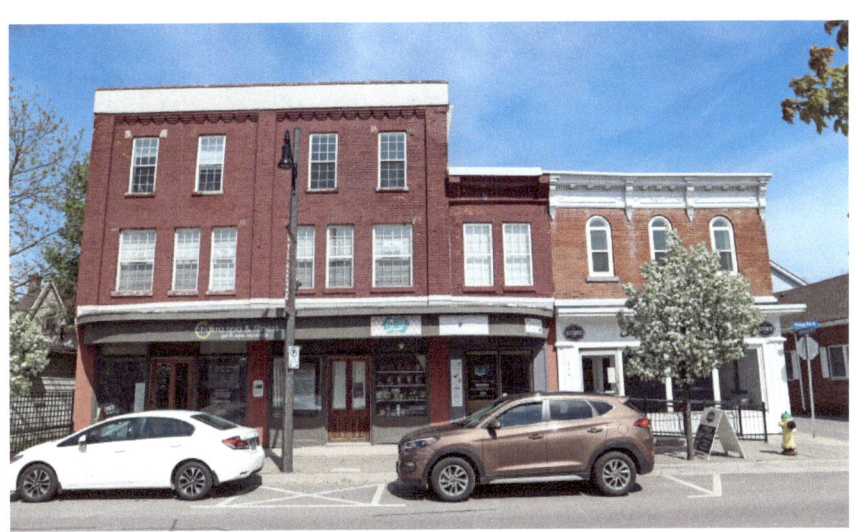

296 Ridge Road North

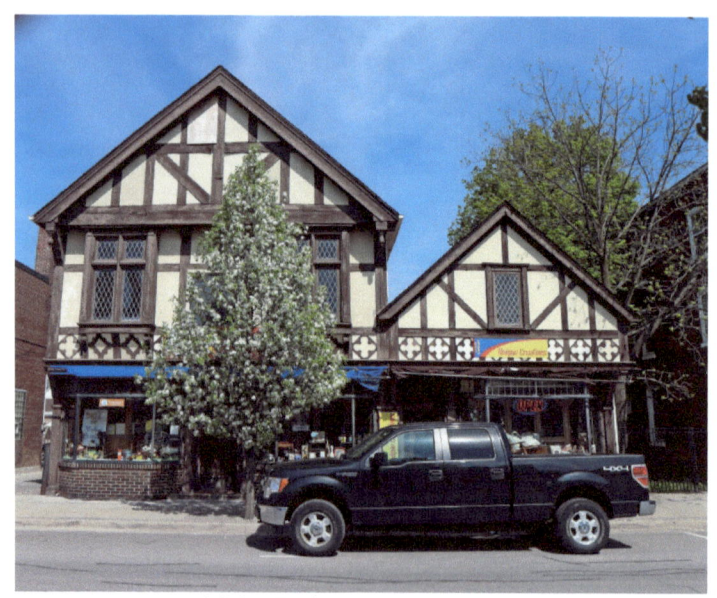

1061 Ridge Road North

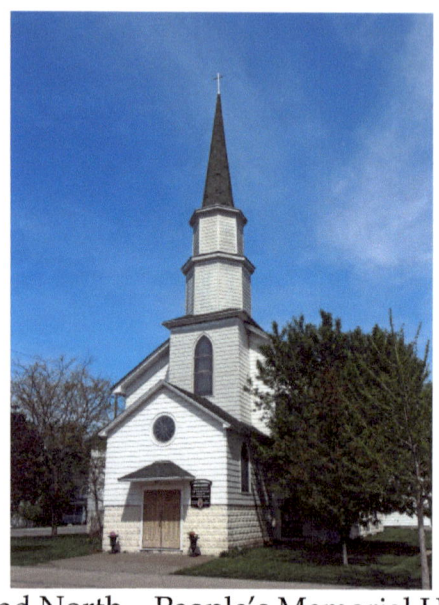

366 Ridge Road North – People's Memorial United Church

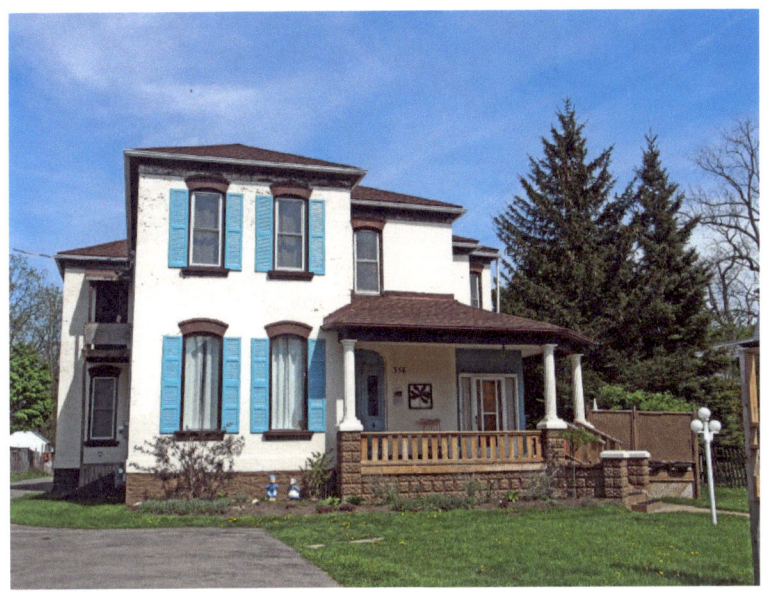

356 Ridge Road North

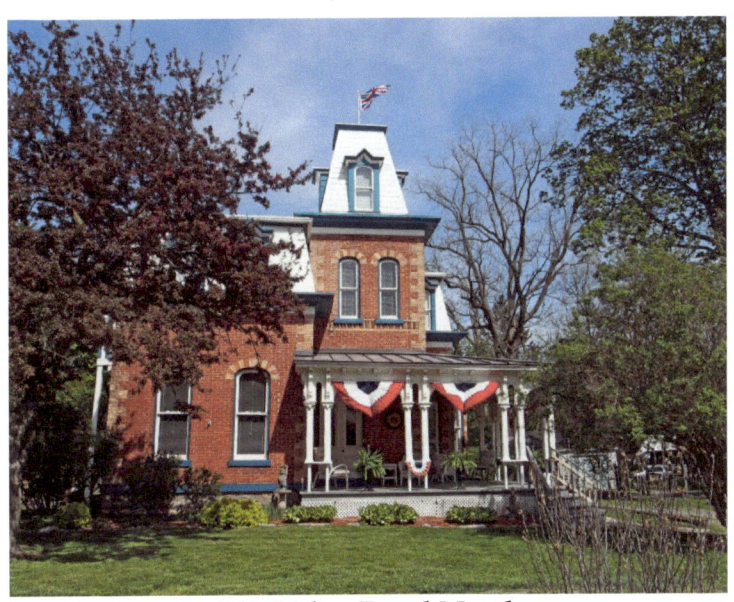

348 Ridge Road North

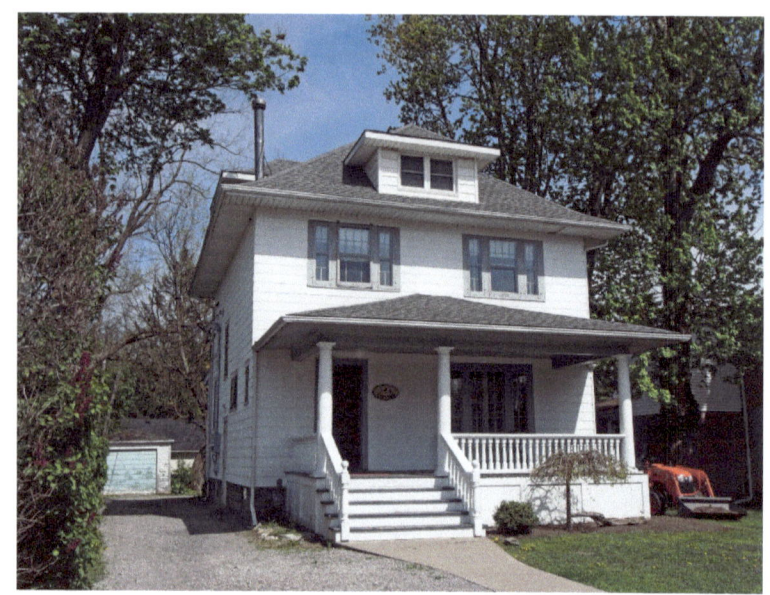

344 Ridge Road North

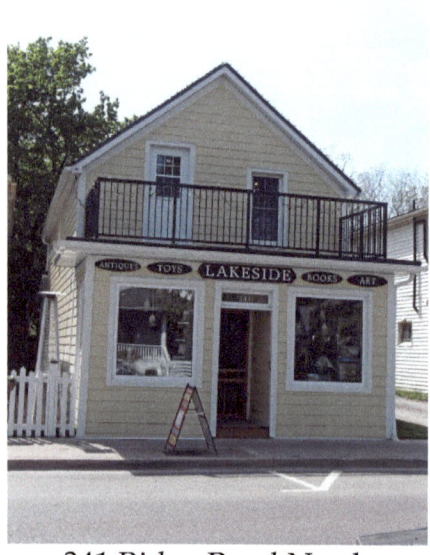

341 Ridge Road North

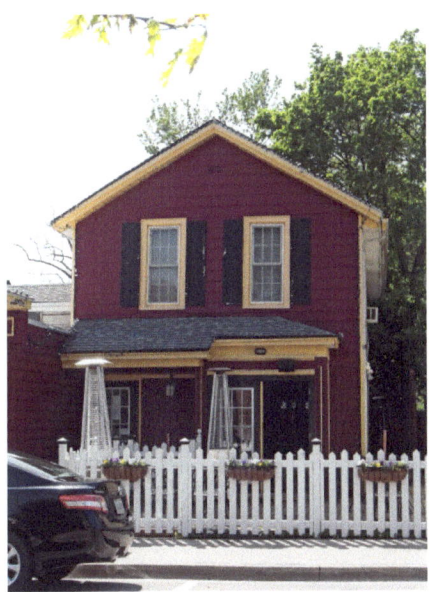

Ridge Road North

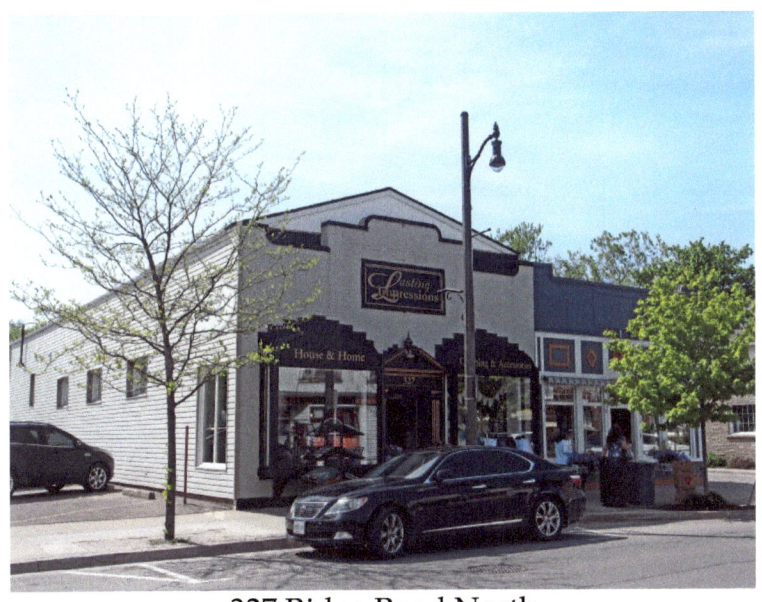

327 Ridge Road North

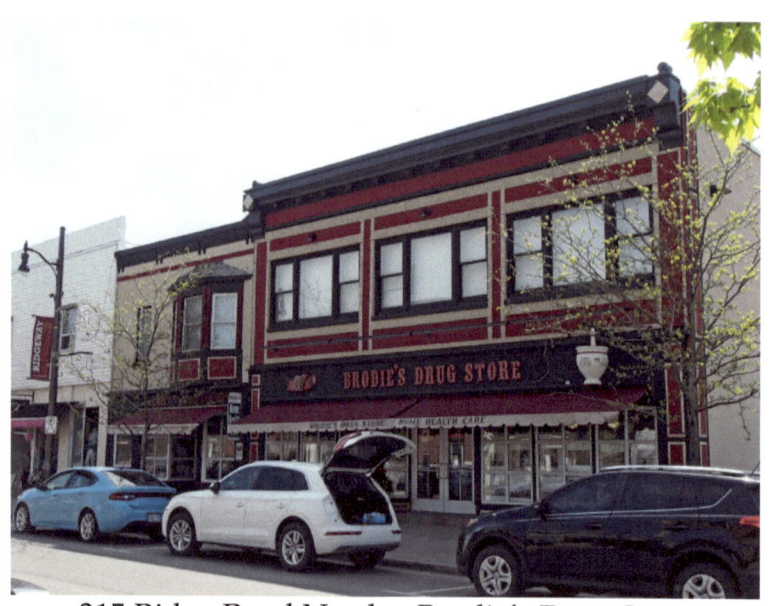
315 Ridge Road North – Brodie's Drug Store

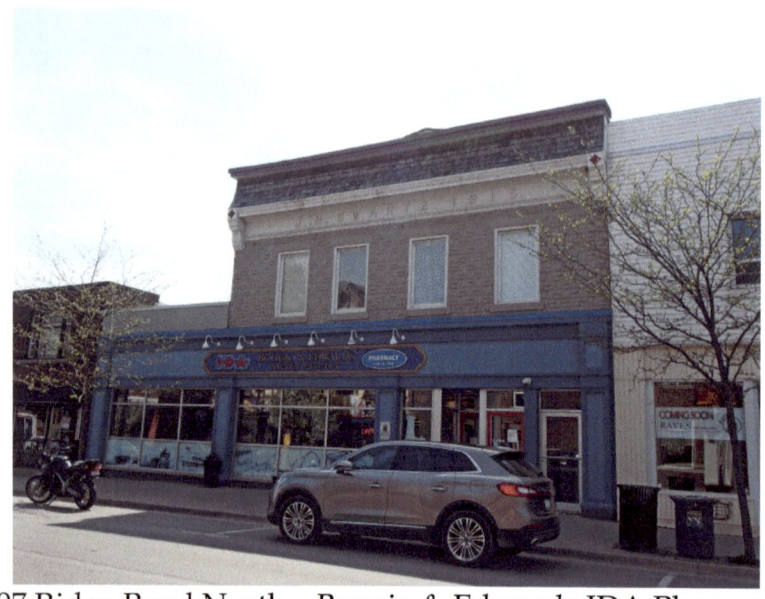
307 Ridge Road North – Boggio & Edwards IDA Pharmacy

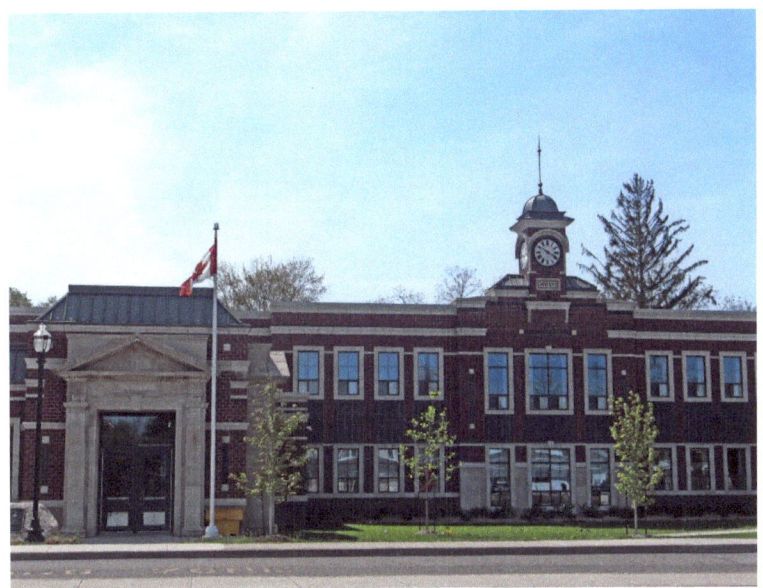

143 Ridge Road North – John Brant Public School

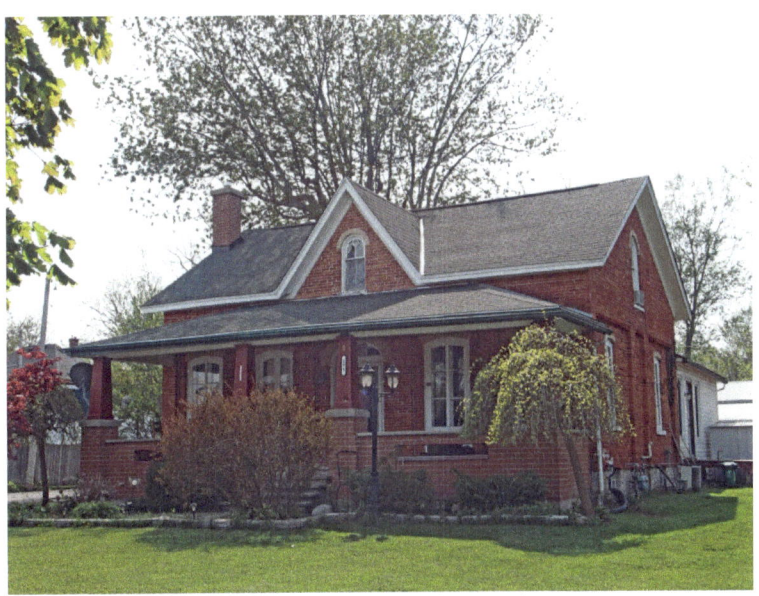

199 Ridge Road North

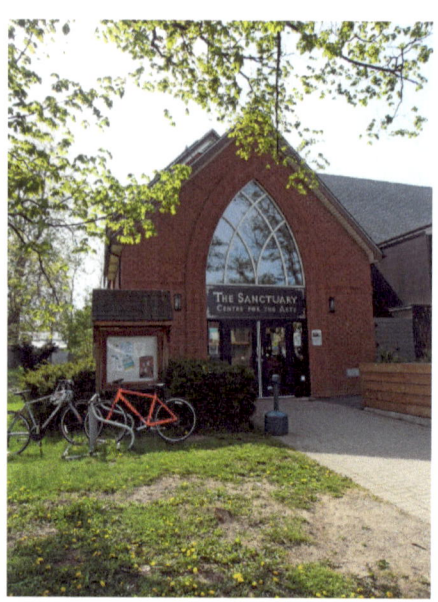

209 Ridge Road North – originally a Free Methodist Church, then Ridgeway Community Church which closed in 2010. It is now *The Sanctuary Centre for the Arts*.

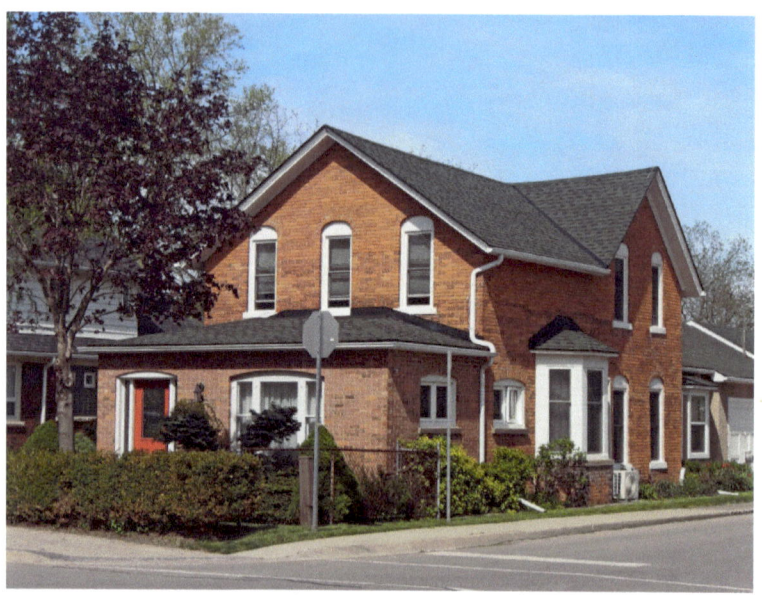

Ridge Road North

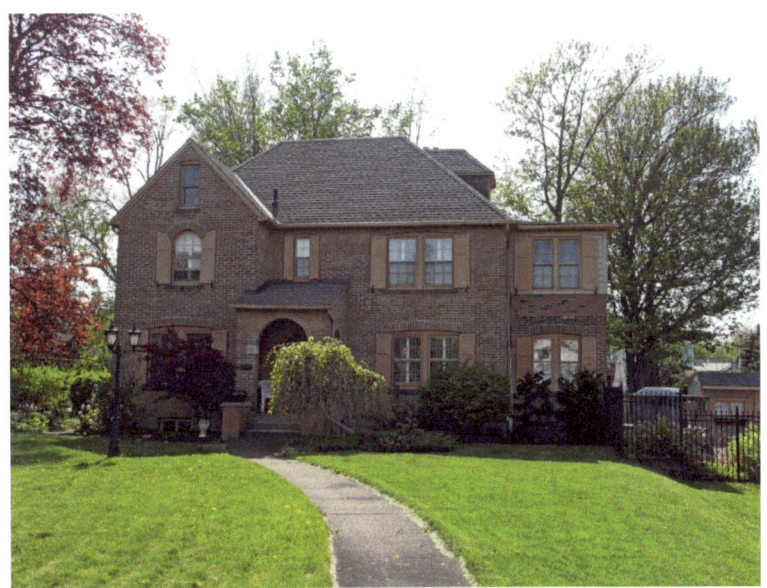

227 Ridge Road North

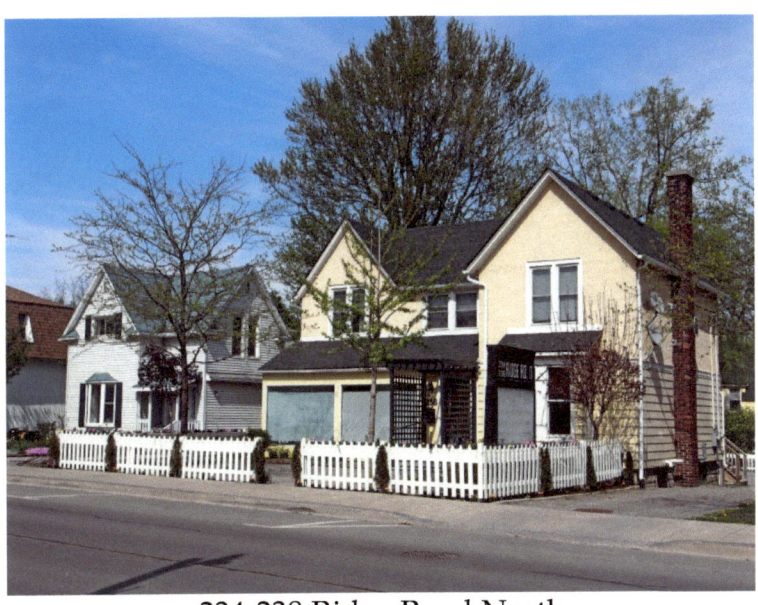

234-238 Ridge Road North

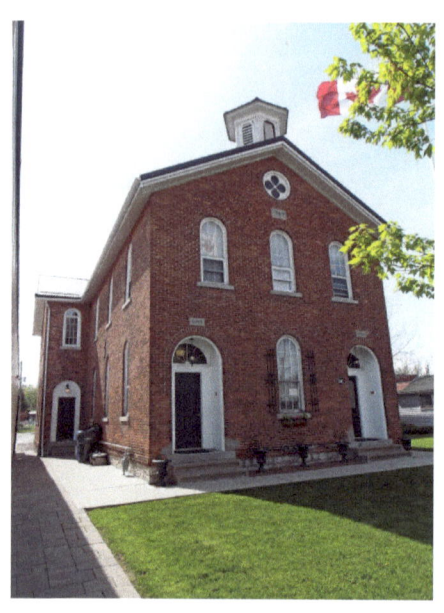

241 Ridge Road North – S.S. No. 11 School - 1869

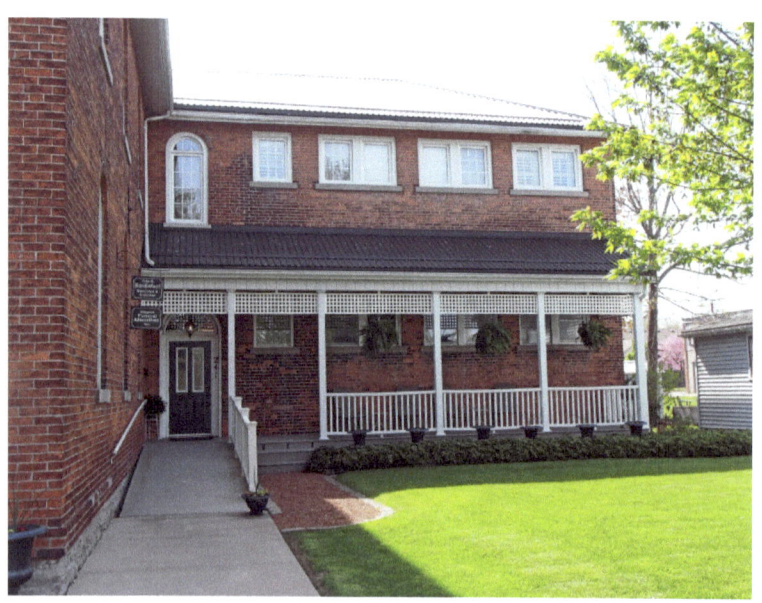

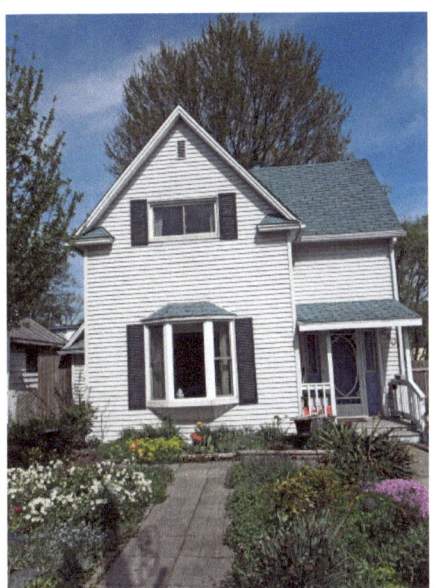

240 Ridge Road North

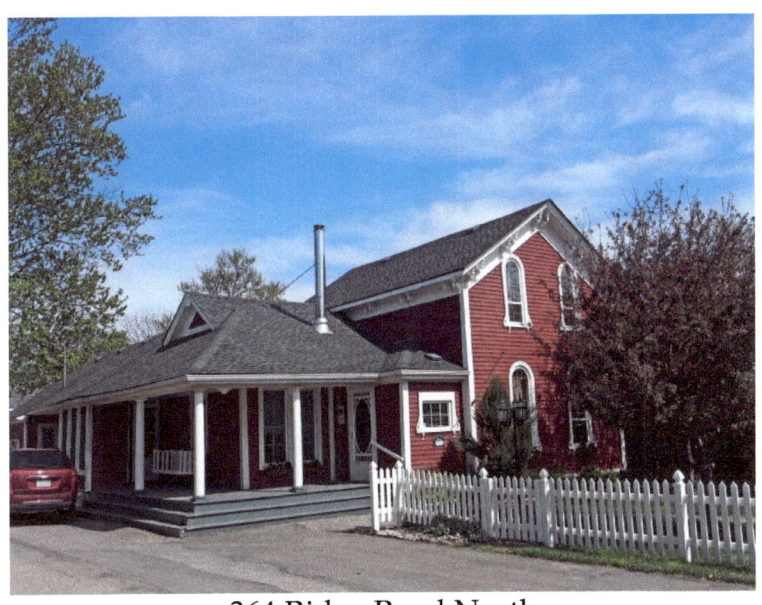

364 Ridge Road North

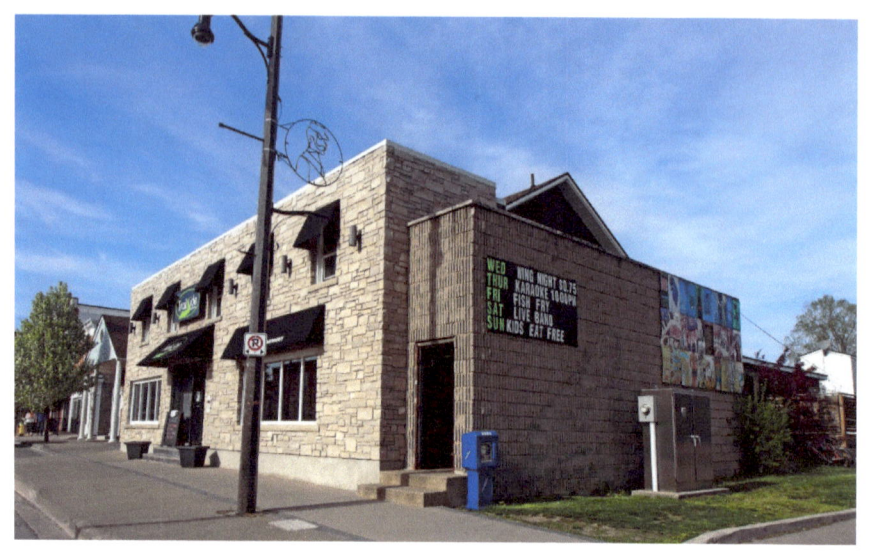

282 Ridge Road North – Trail Side Restaurant

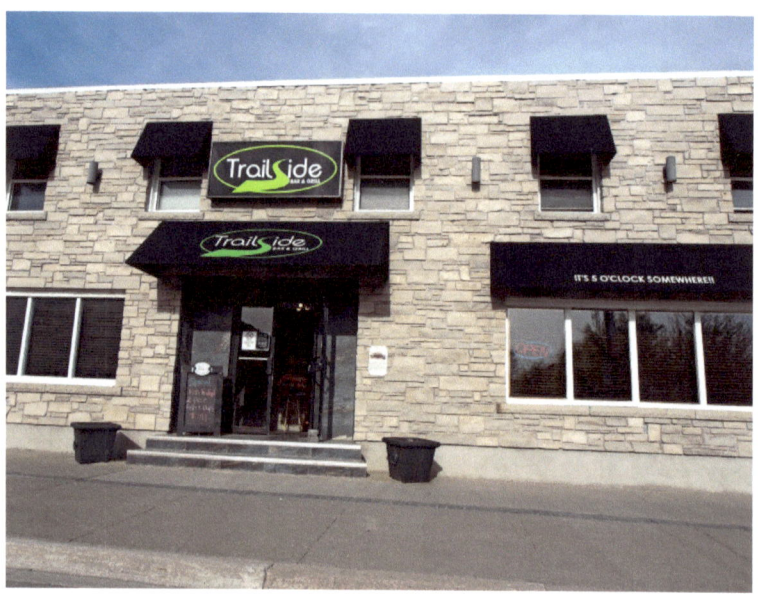

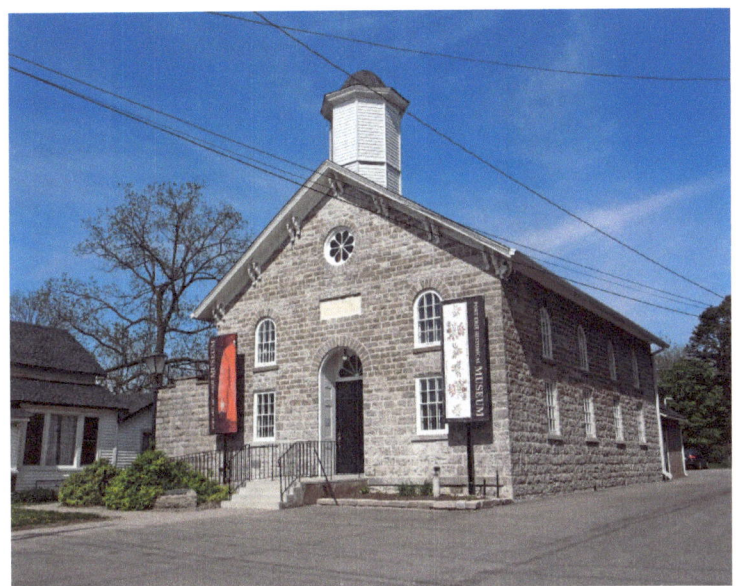

402 Ridge Road North – Fort Erie Historical Museum - The former Bertie Township Municipal Building was constructed in 1874. This Italianate structure was designed to look monumental, solid, and respectable with its round-headed windows and paired brackets at the cornice.

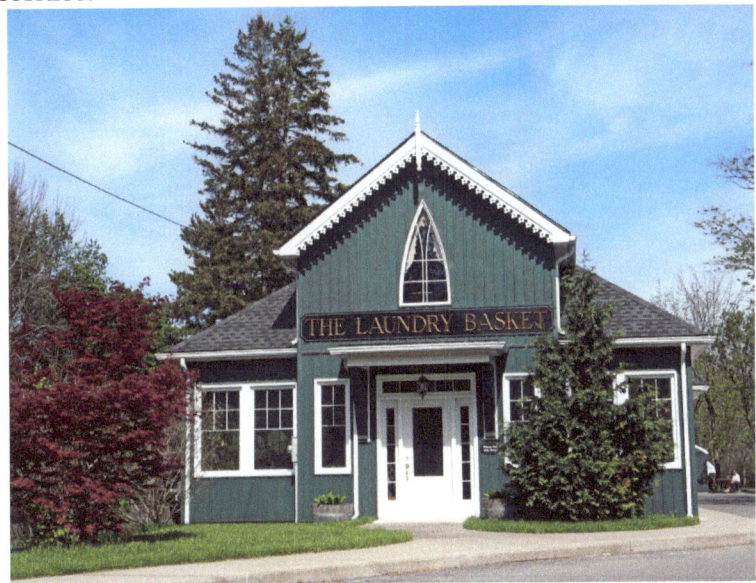

468 Ridge Road North – The Laundry Basket Dry Cleaners

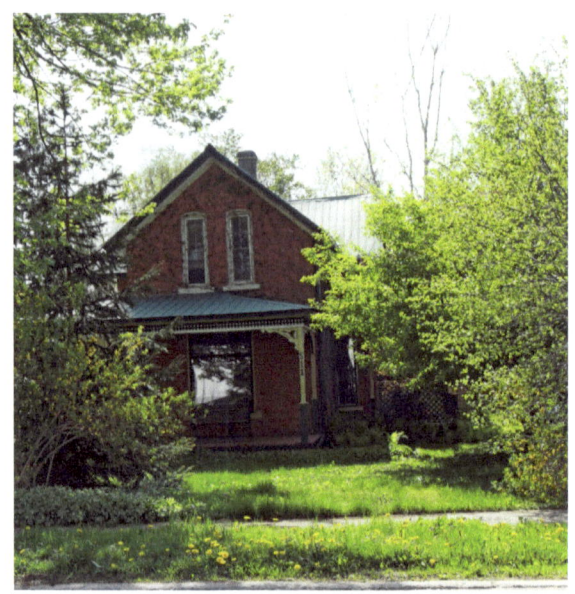

511 Ridge Road North

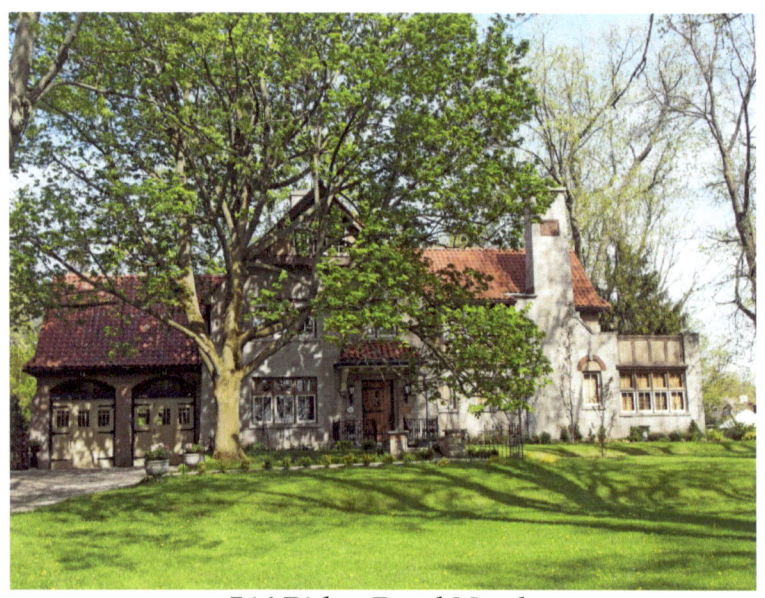

546 Ridge Road North

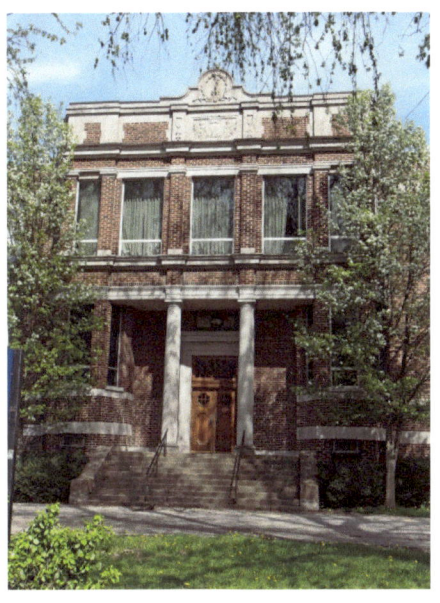

576 Ridge Road North – Ridgeway-Crystal Beach High School

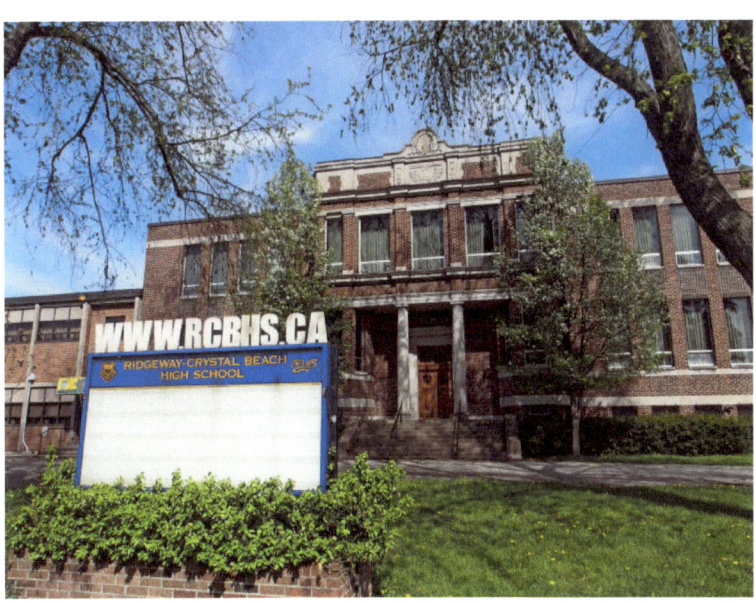

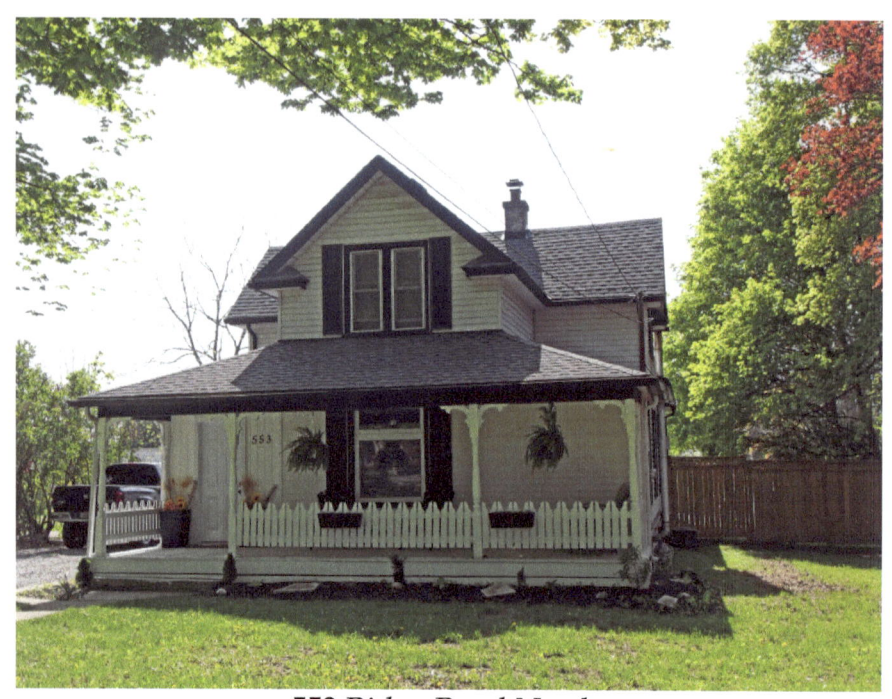

553 Ridge Road North

Stevensville

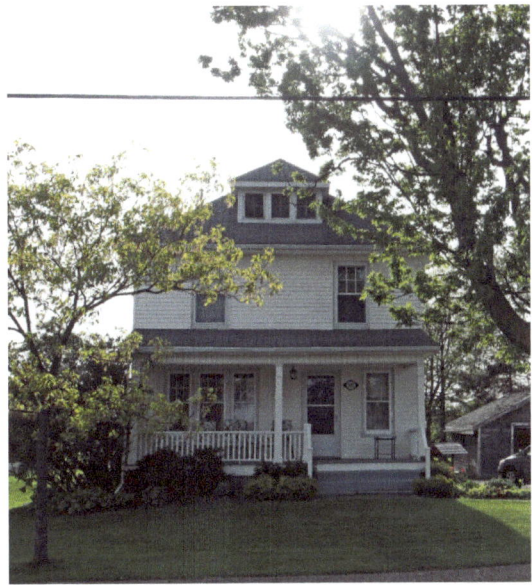

2465 Stevensville Road

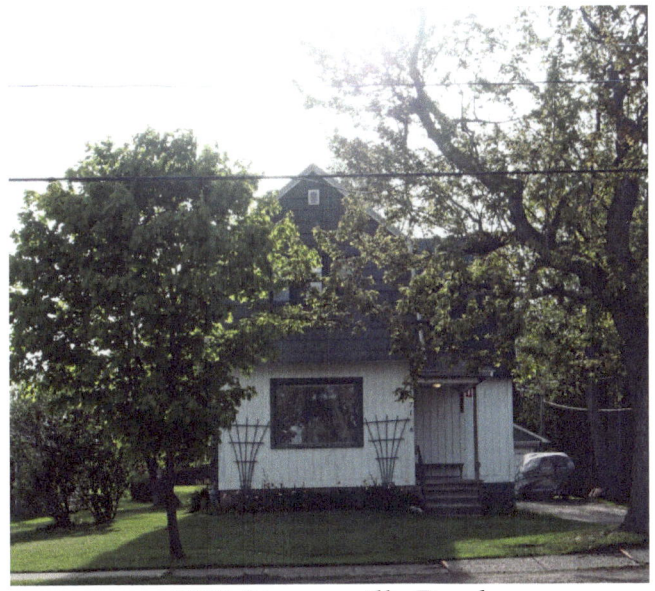

2571 Stevensville Road

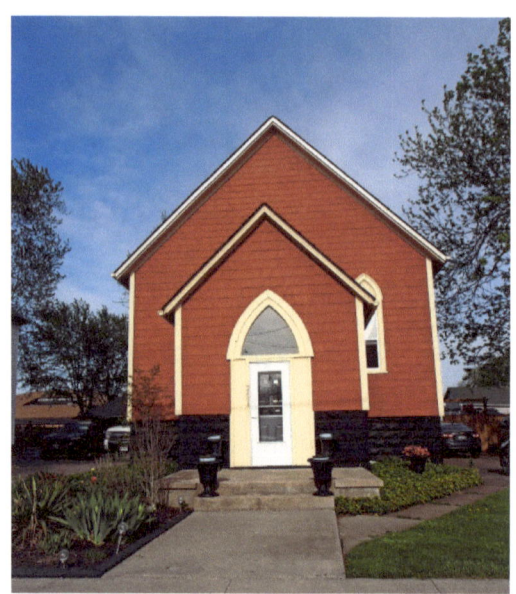

2494 Stevensville Road

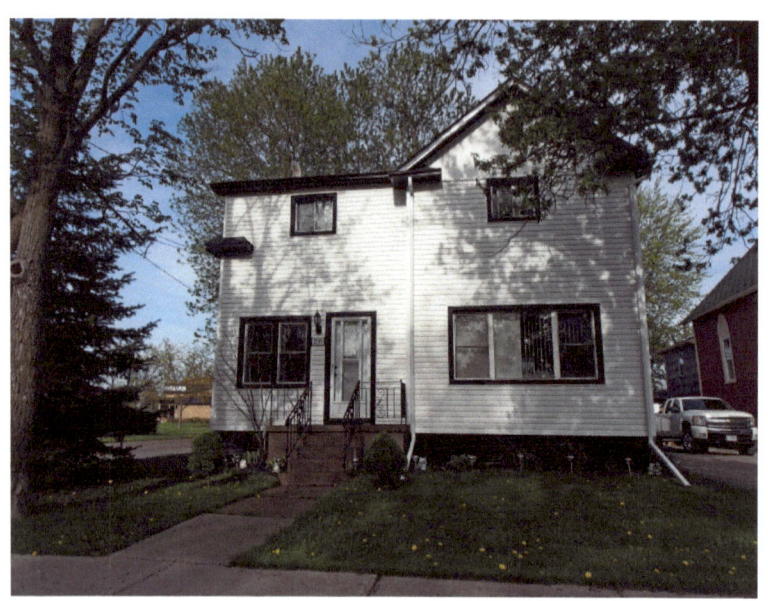

2500 Stevensville Road

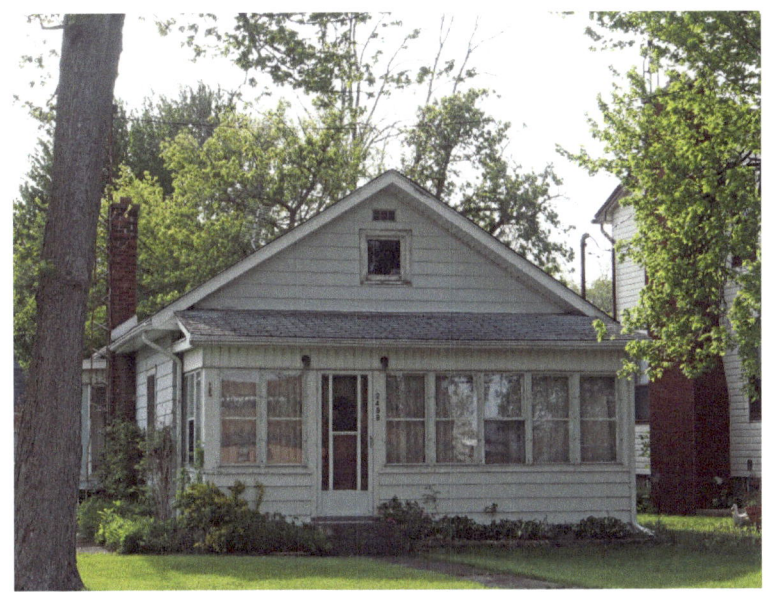

2499 Stevensville Road

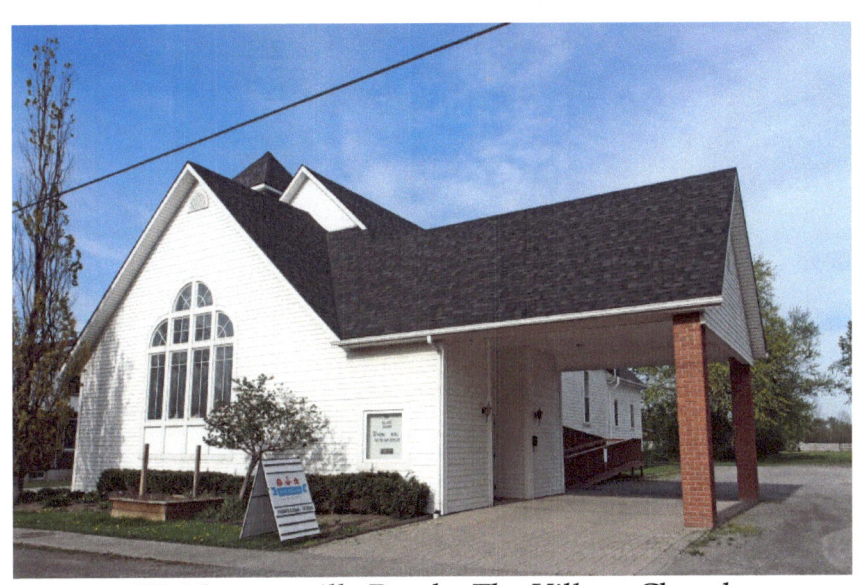

2536 Stevensville Road – The Village Church

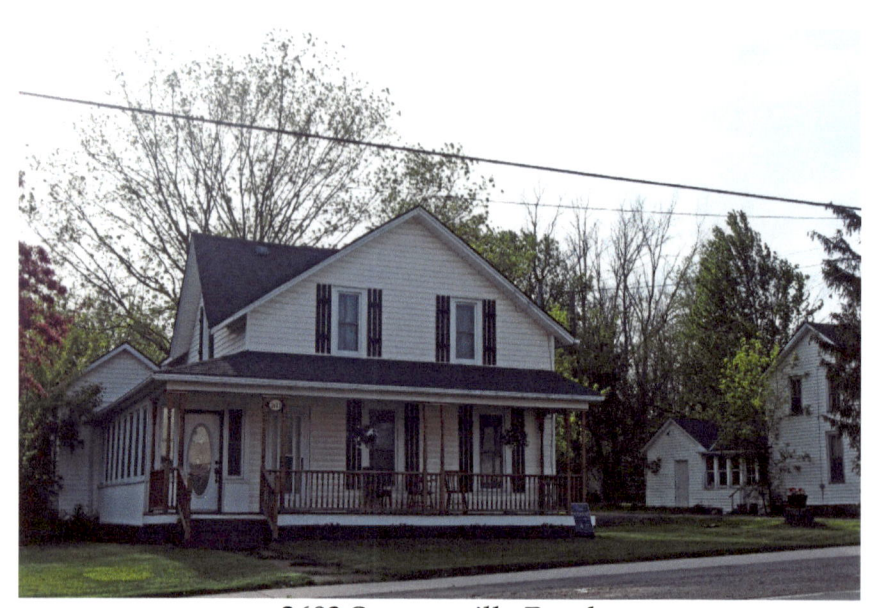

2603 Stevensville Road

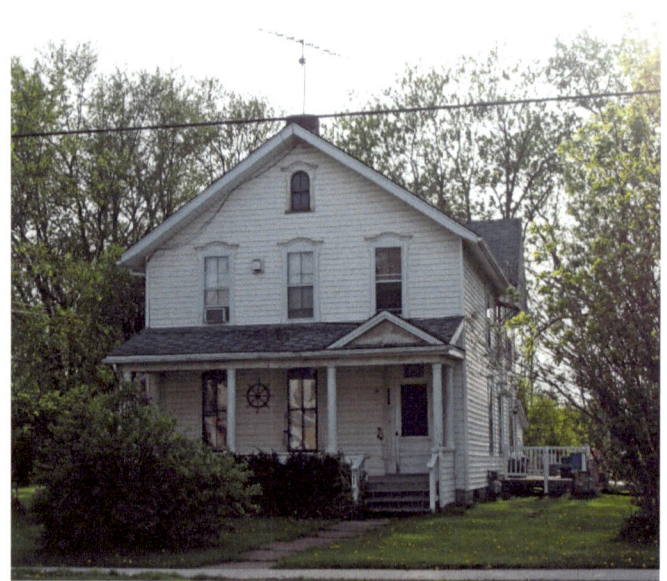

2631 Stevensville Road

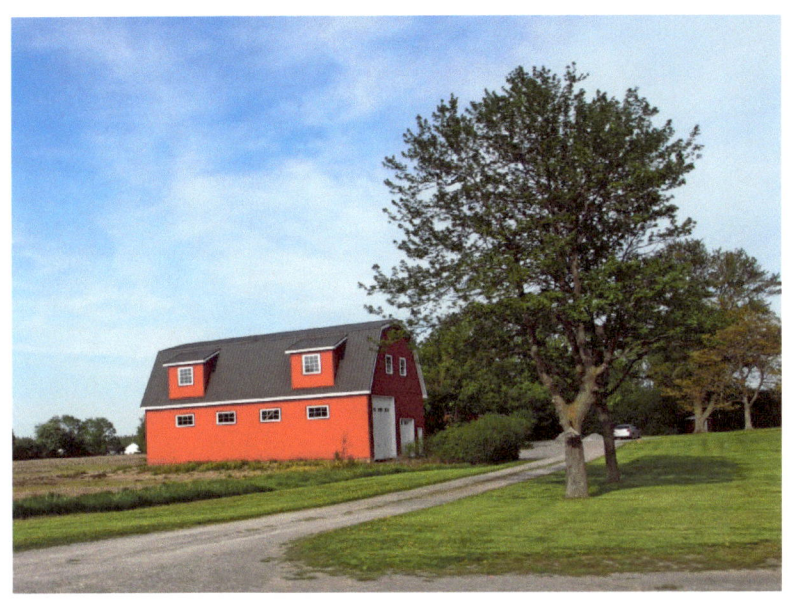

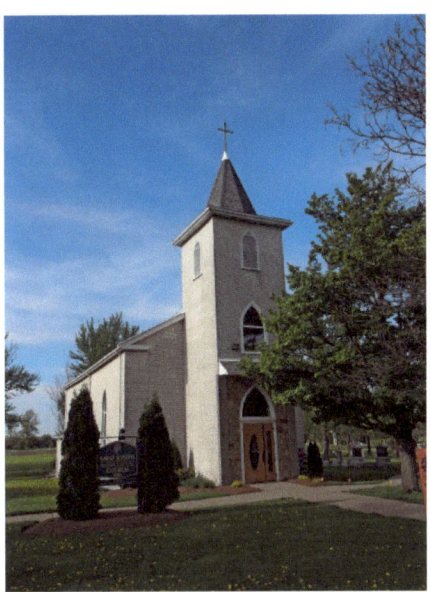

3718 Netherby Road – St. Joseph Roman Catholic Church

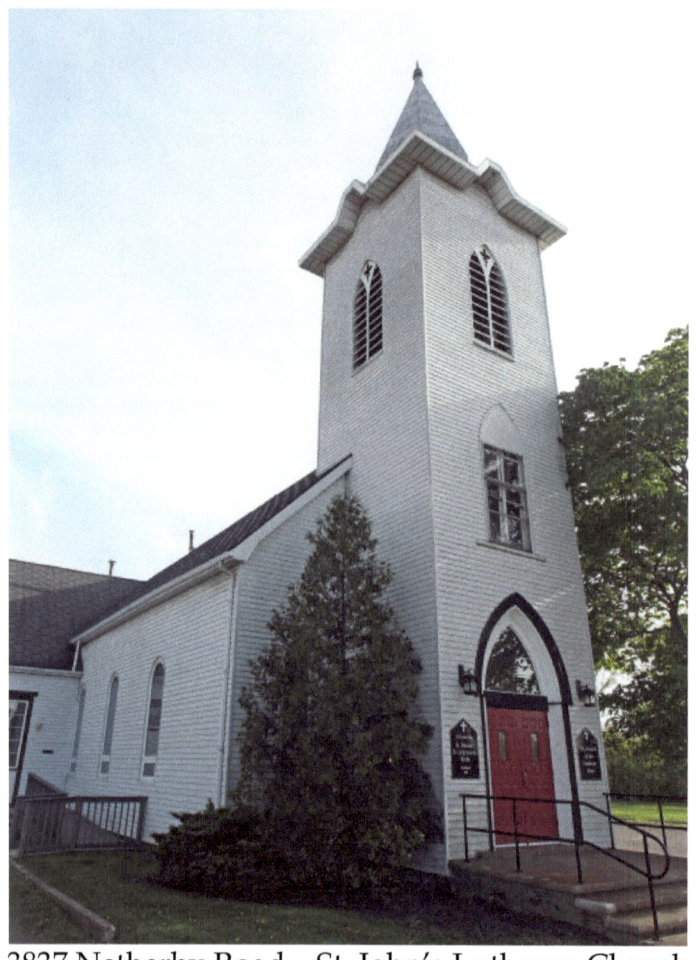

3837 Netherby Road – St. John's Lutheran Church

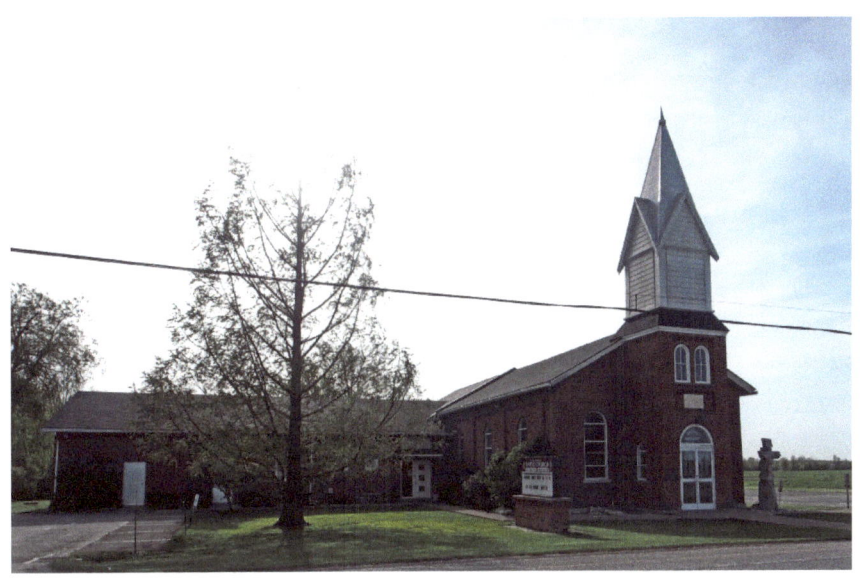

14789 Sodom Road – St. John's Stevensville United Church

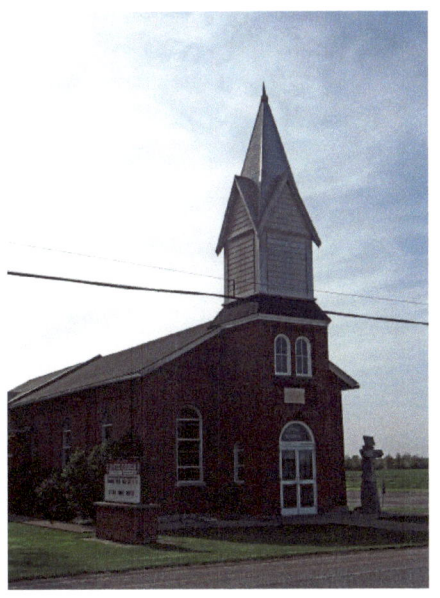

Building Styles

Gothic Revival, 1830-1890 – These decorative buildings have sharply-pitched gables with highly detailed verge boards, pointed-arch window openings, and dichromatic brickwork. It is a common style in Ontario.

Greek Revival – have gabled or hipped roofs with low pitches. The cornice of the main roof usually has a wide band which represents the entablature of classical Greek architecture consisting of the frieze and the architrave. Greek or Roman columns usually support the porch. The front door is surrounded by sidelights and a rectangular transom and is usually dressed with pilasters, pediments and/or columns.

Italianate, 1850-1900 – A two story rectangular building with a mild hip roof, a projecting frontispiece, and generous eaves with ornate cornice brackets was the basis of the style; often there are large sash windows, quoins, ornate detailing on the windows, belvederes and wraparound verandahs. Italianate commercial buildings often have cast iron cresting and elegant window surrounds.

Neo-Gothic (Collegiate Gothic): is monochromatic and on a much grander scale than Gothic. Early Neo-Gothic was the decorative use of Gothic elements with a lack of knowledge and understanding of Gothic construction. Neo-Gothic tried to understand the basic principles of Gothic and used them. Early neo-Gothic churches were often plastered or painted, later neo-Gothic churches were not. An important moment in the development of neo-Gothic is the year 1853, when the hierarchy of the Roman Catholic church was fully restored in the Netherlands. Materials used were natural stone combined with brick. Around the year 1850 neo-Gothicism was maturing and increasingly became a Roman Catholic style almost exclusively. Neo-Gothic was adopted as the style for schools and universities in the early years of the 20th century. The style became so common for scholastic buildings that it is often called Collegiate Gothic. Wall buttresses and finials are added, but they are generally far too small to be of any structural benefit.

Tudor Revival – exposed timbers with stucco infill, multi-paned windows.

Other Books by Barbara Raue

Coins of Gold
Arrows, Indians and Love
The Life and Times of Barbara
The Cromwell Family Book
Laura Secord Discovered
Daddy Where Are You?

Montana Series
Book 1: Montana Dream
Book 2: Life on the Montana Frontier
Book 3: Montana to Boston and Back
Book 4: Montana Sons Go to War
Book 5: Montana Sons Return from War

Donaldson Series
Book 1: Rite of Passage
Book 2: Rite of Marriage

© 2021 by Barbara Raue - All the photos in this book have been taken with my cameras. I own the rights to them.

Barbara is The Authority on Saving Our History One Photo at a Time. She is pursuing her interest in photography and architecture by preserving a record through photos of old buildings from the 1800s and 1900s with their unique architecture. Enjoy the beautiful architecture in the comfort of your living room. Dream about what it was like in those by-gone days. Dream about what it was like to live in a mansion like one of those in this book.

Barbara Raue, a wife, mother and grandmother, is an avid reader and writer. She has researched and compiled several family histories. In 2010, Barbara published her book "Coins of Gold," which celebrates the courageous life of her mother, May Todd. Barbara's second book is a historical fiction "Arrows, Indians and Love" which takes place in Boonesborough, Kentucky during the time of Daniel Boone. In 2013, Barbara published *The Cromwell Family Book* in which she traces her ancestry generations back into Great Britain. Her second novel is called *Laura Secord Discovered,* in which the story of Laura's service during the War of 1812 is shared. Barbara's memoir is titled *Daddy Where Are You?* It tells of her life growing up without a father. Five novels in the Montana Series have been published, *Montana Dream, Life on the Montana Frontier, Montana to Boston and Back, Montana Sons Go to War*, and *Montana Sons Return from War*. The Donaldson series of two novels is available: *Rite of Passage* and *Rite of Marriage*.

This is a link to Barbara's website to view all of her books
http://barbararaue.ca

www.ingramcontent.com/pod-product-compliance
Lightning Source LLC
Chambersburg PA
CBHW040246220526
45473CB00001B/385